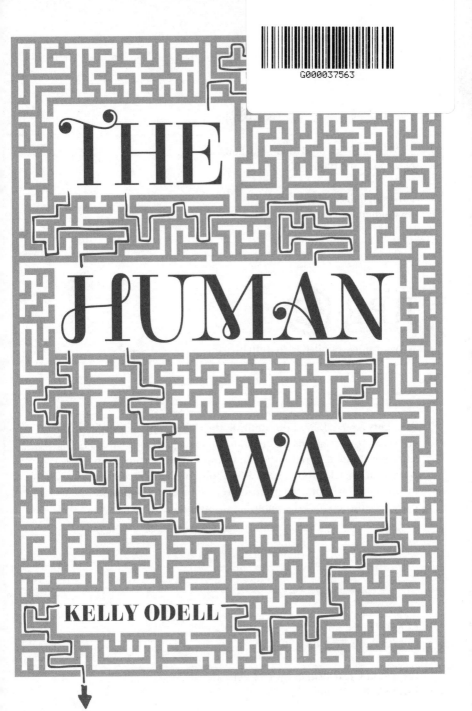

THE HUMAN WAY

KELLY ODELL

The Ten Commandments
for (Im)Perfect Leaders

Published by
LID Publishing Ltd.
One Adam Street, London. WC2N 6LE

31 West 34th St., 8th Floor, Suite 8004
New York, NY 10001, US

info@lidpublishing.com
www.lidpublishing.com

A member of:

B P R
Business Publishers Roundtable
www.businesspublishersroundtable.com

Printed in Great Britain by TJ International
ISBN: 978-1-910649-67-1

Cover and page design: Caroline Li

THE HUMAN WAY

The Ten Commandments for (Im)Perfect Leaders

KELLY ODELL

LONDON   MONTERREY
MADRID   SHANGHAI
MEXICO CITY   BOGOTA
NEW YORK   BUENOS AIRES
BARCELONA   SAN FRANCISCO

CONTENTS

INTRODUCTION

Anyone who wants to be a better manager can be. This book is intended for anyone who strives to be more successful in their leadership role; anyone who has read all the books on leadership and taken all the courses; and for anyone who has tested various theories around leadership, and maybe even come up with a few of their own.

Much of what is conveyed in today's leadership literature, and in leadership training, is, at best, only knowledge about leadership. The aim of this book is to focus on *how* to think about leadership, rather than on *what* we should think or do. *How* we think about people, motivation, power and relationships is actually more important than *what* we think. As leaders, our values – and how we view other people, the purpose of the organization and our own roles – are the key to our success. This knowledge affects what we learn and how we use what we have learned. Knowledge about leadership is constantly growing and developing, but our approach to leadership should stay relatively stable.

Experience over the years, and research, has helped us gain a better understanding of how to improve our communication skills, how to manage our resources better and how to create an enhanced climate for employee engagement. This type of knowledge helps us to develop our skills so we can be more effective as leaders and managers. But what ultimately defines us as managers has more to do with our world view – or *weltanschauung* in German, as we called it in philosophy class – than with our specific skills as leaders. Our world view will define the skills we believe to be important, the information we seek, the challenges upon which we focus and those we ignore.

When I began my career as a manager, I discovered I held strong beliefs about the organization and my role within it. These beliefs had a significant impact on my success as a manager. I refer to these notions as "beliefs" because, when I began to reflect on them, I couldn't find any real analytical foundation underpinning why I believed these notions to be true. It became clear that, in order to be successful as a manager, I would have to re-evaluate much of what I believed to be true about organizations and the roles of the people in them.

The following is a list of questions that influenced my world view as a manager:

- What is the purpose of the organization, or organizations in general?
- What is the definition of success for me as a person and for the organization as a whole?
- What are the roles of managers, leaders, staff and others in these organizations?
- What are the relationships between these individual roles in achieving the purpose of the organization?

Even more fundamental were the questions around whom I was (or who I wanted to be) and what I wanted to achieve in my life.

As I struggled with these questions, I began to gain a clearer understanding of the challenges facing us as managers in organizations. This book is one of the outcomes of this process. It will likely raise more questions than answers for the reader. Ultimately, growth begins with questions. As leaders, we must continuously question and re-evaluate the things we believe to be true. Sometimes, the results of these reflections confirm that we are on the right track. Other times, we discover we are on the wrong path. Either one of these insights is important. The only way to know whether you are headed in the right direction is to look around frequently and view the landscape. All too often, managers are so busy with their operational responsibilities, they simply don't take the time to stop and reflect.

This book is built around 'ten commandments' which have their origins in one of my most popular lectures. When I give a lecture, it is fairly common for me to be introduced as the 'preacher-turned-businessman'. This is only partly true. As a young man, I spent four years studying theology at the University of Oklahoma and Phillips University in the US, in preparation for a career in the ministry that never actually happened. In short, I am not ordained and have never worked as a minister.

The concept behind my 'ten commandments' was simply that it would be a fun way of organizing the content of a lecture on leadership, but the content of these commandments is the result of many years of study, reflection and practical experience as a leader. I struggled with my own leadership ability in various management positions. I also struggled with the leadership of my superiors.

Over time, I began to discover various elements that seemed to be critical in leadership. I discovered that some factors seemed to transcend variations in organizational cultures, or differences in individual personalities. The essence of good leadership did not seem to lie in particular activities or behaviors, good leadership seemed to stem from something else. This is not to say that there are not a great many good and bad behaviors or activities that we can learn, or learn to exclude from our management skills. But what seemed more important were the values behind our behaviors.

In fact, strong values guiding a leader can compensate for a number of poor behavioral habits. For example, I have worked with leaders who never really got around to annual performance reviews. I would probably agree that properly executed reviews are a positive activity. But some of the managers who didn't undertake formal performance reviews were some of the best leaders I have worked with. Looking back, I realize I was never in doubt about what they thought of my performance, or what I needed to focus on to improve. These managers were so 'in the now', or present, in the daily lives of their organizations and their people that, in effect, we had informal performance reviews all the time.

These managers might have been even better had they held formal, structured, and frequent performance reviews, but their strong values compensated for certain behavioral weaknesses.

By contrast, I have had managers who were poor leaders, despite doing everything by the book. They really didn't seem to care about the people they were leading and/or didn't strive to understand the real purpose of the organization, or their role as manager. They held fast to the faulty assumption that their jobs as managers were simply about executing a series of pre-defined activities: kickoff – check; weekly team meeting – check; performance review – check; and so on. I have come to realize that success as a manager is, first and foremost, a question of *being* – and only secondly about *doing*. If we do not understand who we are, this has a profound impact both on what we choose to do, and ultimately, how we do these things.

I have never met anyone who intentionally wanted to be a bad boss. That said, there are many 'bad bosses' out there, and I am sure I have been one of them, on occasion. You might say a primary thesis of this book is that all bosses are bad bosses from time to time. None of us is perfect. Perfection is not even the goal. I would argue that no-one even knows what perfection in leadership or management even looks like. The goal for every manager is to strive to improve, in the face of their idiosyncrasies, positive and negative. My ten commandments were born out of my own struggle to grow and develop as a leader.

Unlike the original ten commandments, in the *Old Testament* of the *Bible*, my commandments are not rigid, unbending rules, commands or obligations. They should be seen more as a description of an approach to leadership. I know, for certain, that none of us will succeed in following these commandments in every situation, but if we can manage to maintain the approach and the values they reflect, we will succeed more often, and find it easier to cope with those situations in which we do not succeed.

My ten commandments for leaders have grown out of a concept I have chosen to call "human leadership", developed over the course of many years. The idea behind human leadership came to me after I realized I could not live up to the ideal of how a good leader should 'be' – at least, I could not meet all the ideals and demands that leadership training courses and books on the subject deem important. Even today, leadership training courses and literature commonly describe how to lead as if it were a recipe. The assumption is that if you follow the advice they give, step by step, you can expect to achieve the right outcome.

It may well be that if you follow a recipe for making pancakes you will always end up with perfect pancakes, but if you think there is such a thing as a recipe for successful leadership, you had better stay in the kitchen.

Essentially, leadership is a question of relationships, and we all know relationships can be challenging. Perhaps that's why simple answers are so popular. You often read magazine headlines pledging "Three steps to successful leadership" or "Five steps to a happier marriage". Although there are plenty of tips and advice to help us improve our relationships, we all understand there is no recipe for success as a leader – or in a marriage. It cannot be boiled down to three, five or even ten steps.

I would like to offer the same warning when it comes to this book. This is not a leadership cookbook. Rather, I aim to help leaders, as well as employees, improve their approach to leadership, in order to create better conditions for successful leadership. The individual himself or herself has to adapt his or her leadership to each specific situation and circumstance, and to each person, based on his or her own abilities.

Regarding management, someone once said, "if you find yourself doing the same thing twice, then one of them is probably wrong." This book can help us gain a better understanding of the terrain we will be navigating, but we have to choose the destination and the route ourselves. The main theme of the book is that no-one is perfect and success as a leader is not about always doing the right thing. It is about accepting our own humanity and adopting a number of down-to-earth attitudes and values. That's when we achieve true success.

As a young manager, I had trouble articulating what I meant, but I wanted those people working for me to feel that what we were doing was interesting and fun, and that together, we could arrive at a positive outcome. In achieving this, my managers and colleagues would think I was good at what I did, and as time went on, I would be given new challenges as a leader.

I took leadership training courses, met leadership gurus and read a great deal of the available literature about leadership. However, the more I learned about leadership, the more disenchanted I became in my own abilities. This wasn't because I was failing. We were achieving good results, and in employee surveys, it was clear that my staff liked me and the way we worked. I was promoted, and my bosses were happy with my work. All the outward signs seemed to indicate that I was a good leader, but I still felt inadequate.

I worked hard to do the right thing, the way I had learned to do it, but I still made mistakes and failed once in a while. I would get stressed and forget things, and even if I had good days, I was not always at the top of my game. Despite my blunders, I was achieving good results. But...

I could not meet the theoretical expectations of how a good leader should be. That's where I failed.

As a result, I began to understand that the problem with many of today's theories about leadership is that they place unrealistic demands both on the people who act as leaders and on those who follow them. Certain theories about leadership are purely utopian in their expectations of how people function. They paint a picture in which the leader should set a good example and become a role model, but where does it say that the leader is also just a human being?

It also became increasingly obvious to me that managers and leaders are not the same things. I began to realize that you can be a manager without being a leader and you can be a leader without being a manager. Although it is ideal to have a manager who is also a leader, unfortunately, this is not always the case. The position of manager is a formal role in an organization, but to become a leader, someone has to follow you. I will take a closer look at this later on in the book.

Anyway, if you accept the assertion that a leader or manager is still a human being, you realize that leaders and managers are no better, nor worse, than anyone else. A leader is human, and there are people in leadership roles who are better, others who are worse. Some people are prepared to sacrifice their lives to improve the world. Others don't care about their fellow human beings; their behavior can be extremely egotistical or even criminal. But most of us fall somewhere in between. The same goes for our leaders. Some have high moral standards, others very low standards, with the vast majority of leaders somewhere in between. I think we can agree on this.

I would like to make it clear that it is possible to be a good leader without having positive intentions.

A person can possess excellent leadership qualities, and have many followers, without being a decent person. Their agenda might actually be very negative – even evil – but they may still be a good leader. For example, it could be argued that Hitler was an excellent leader. He was successful in gathering a great number of followers and rallying them around a common purpose but his intent was clearly evil.

For argument's sake, let's assume that the head of an organization is also perceived to be a leader and has positive intentions in that role. Although most of us realize leaders and managers are not perfect, we still expect them to set a good example and to act as a role model. But if this leader is just an ordinary person, with strengths and weaknesses like everyone else in the organization, why should this person be expected to be better than anyone else?

A more reasonable perspective would be to assume that everyone in the organization strives to be a role model for one another, but to be realistic and understand that sometimes things don't work out that way. A leadership model based on the premise that the leader is better than his or her staff is doomed to failure. If you assume leaders do everything right, or at least make fewer mistakes, you will be disappointed. And we certainly do grow disillusioned when our leaders demonstrate their failings. In fact, we react much more strongly when our leaders make mistakes than when non-leaders mess up.

If a manager is not better than his or her team members, what separates the two? The only difference is the roles they play within the organization and their work responsibilities. So I asked myself "how could an ordinary person like me, with all my weaknesses and faults, be a good leader?" I decided that the premise that leaders are people with faults and weaknesses – who have a tough time living up to expectations of perfection – might be a key to developing a lasting and sustainable leadership model.

If organizations, and the people within them, took a more realistic view of leadership, and allowed leaders to be human, this would generate far less disappointment among employees and create greater organizational success.

When I travel and speak to groups of employees and ask "do you think your managers' live up to the expectations you have of them?" about two-thirds are usually unimpressed by their managers. If I pose the same question to a group of managers, roughly two-thirds feel their managers meet, or exceed, their expectations. So I wondered why non-managers are tougher in judging their bosses than those who manage/lead teams or organizations. I arrived at the conclusion that managers have respect for, and an understanding of, managerial problems, and thus are more forgiving in judging their superiors. But non-managers sometimes have unreasonable expectations about what their leaders should be able to handle. Some people feel that a manager should be better at doing a non-manager's job than the individual themselves and should be able to address all problems that are encountered in the workplace.

To address this, I started to develop the term 'human leadership'. My intention was to build leadership models that incorporate realistic, and 'human' demands. I don't mean that we should lower our standards, only that we should dispense with the traditional, standard perception of how a leader should be, and instead make our demands more reasonable.

If we look back on history, kings, dictators, generals and religious leaders have ruled with absolute power. The best that ordinary people could hope for was that these leaders would wield their power with intelligence and benevolence. But the history books are filled with as many examples of tyrannical leaders as excellent ones, and the majority of leaders throughout history fall into the 'mediocre' category.

Over the years, I have come to realize that a bad manager can cause more damage for his or her organization and for team members, than a good manager can create value. When an organization is running well, a manager can create conditions that enable employees to enjoy their work and be productive, but ultimately the manager is only one human resource creating value. By contrast, a bad manager can effectively prevent many employees from doing their work and severely undermine their motivation.

In a well-run organization, it is the ordinary members of personnel, the non-managers, who create most of the value, while in companies with poor leadership, it is the manager who prevents value from being created.

As managers, we may not always succeed in creating attractive visions of the future and inspiring people to do great things, but if we also avoid creating the hurdles that undermine staff morale, motivation and creativity, the organization will still generate great value. Given that most of us managers are ordinary, middle-of-the-road types, we just have to accept the fact that if good leadership were crucial to success, few of our businesses would be as successful as they are.

If I could dispel one single myth about leadership, it would be the myth around what I call the "hero leader". We humans love our heroes; perhaps we even need heroic figures as role models to inspire us and give us hope. I have read a great deal of what has been written about many key leaders throughout history. In my youth, I devoured biographies of great leaders in the hope of uncovering a few kernels of wisdom revealing what makes a leader successful.

One thing became very clear to me, and that was that almost all of these highly successful leaders were in the right place at the right time. In other words, outside circumstances had a great deal to do with their success.

Growing up, I learned that former US presidents George Washington and Abraham Lincoln were great leaders, and I don't doubt that they were. But what if George Washington had not been alive when the US declared its *Declaration of Independence* and launched a revolution against England? Had he been born in another era, he might still have been elected president, but it is unlikely that the common man would still know his name.

Abraham Lincoln was a relatively unsuccessful politician up until he was elected president. Based on what I have read, I believe he was a highly intelligent person with a popular, down-to-earth manner, a gifted speaker, and undoubtedly, a good leader. But imagine if he had not won the election? Imagine if someone else had been president during the American Civil War? The north would, in all likelihood, have won, because of its military might and superior access to natural resources, industry and finances. Slavery would no doubt have been abolished anyway, if not then, fairly soon thereafter. Other people would have made other decisions and history would have looked different – but not that different.

Don't get me wrong. I think both George Washington and Abraham Lincoln were excellent leaders, worthy of all the praise heaped upon them. But you cannot disregard the fact that there were perhaps other gifted leaders who could have achieved just as much, if not more. Ultimately, it was far more important for history that there was strong popular support for the American Revolution and Civil War than the fact that Washington and Lincoln were good leaders.

If you look at the growth of a modern company, you can see that the success of many of them – maybe even most of them – has been the result of innovative inventions or business concepts. Ingvar Kamprad had an idea and a new way of selling home furnishings, and IKEA would not have become what it is today without him, but neither would it have been successful without the help of all the skilled people around him. The key factor in IKEA's success has been Kamprad's entrepreneurial abilities rather than his leadership skills.

Kamprad's outstanding head for business was apparent, even as a child of five, when he purchased matches in bulk in Stockholm, selling them individually in his local area, within the forests of southern Sweden. I would argue that Ingvar, as he is lovingly known in Sweden, never had a particular passion for furniture, or for any of the other things he has sold throughout his life. He has a passion for business, whether it be seeds, kitchen tables or nylon stockings (all of which he has sold during his career). I have no reason to doubt his leadership, but that is not why IKEA became IKEA.

To summarize: a leader is not unimportant, but a leader is not as all-important as we are often led to believe.

If you allow an organization to operate with great openness and trust, people within it will always find the leaders they need when they need them.

These leaders will also be replaced when they no longer satisfy their function, because a variety of different skill sets are needed for a business to succeed; leadership is just one of them, and it is neither more, nor less, important than the others.

LEADERSHIP

is a SKILL

I t is a common belief that some people *are* leaders. In a 2012 study of 361 top-level executives from 53 countries, by the Center for Creative Leadership, 19% of respondents stated that leaders are born to lead, while 52% believed that leaders are created; 29% said that both factors are equally important. I am among those who do not believe a person is born a leader. Certainly, a person can be born with traits that make him or her more prone to be a good leader, but that is not enough to be a good leader. Of course, it doesn't hurt to be born into the right family. The chances of someone becoming the head of a major corporation increase substantially if their father is the head of a major corporation. But, as I have already mentioned, and will argue further later on, the fact that you have become a manager does not guarantee that you will become a leader.

Leadership is a skill, similar to playing a musical instrument. Clearly, some are born with more musical talent than others. In fact, there may well be a few special individuals born every generation who can write a symphony at the age of three, but there are not enough of these gifted individuals to assemble even one orchestra. By the same token, there may be a few special individuals with natural leadership ability, who don't need to learn anything at all (although I doubt that). The problem is that there are not enough of them to fill all the management positions in all of our organizations.

Even if you are born with a natural gift, you still need to work hard to develop it. But, I would wager that a person with fewer natural talents, who strives to improve and is willing to work hard, will go further than a more talented person without drive or ambition. Then there are people who are naturally gifted, ambitious and who also work hard. These types of individual are few and far between. At any rate, there are not enough of them to run our companies or become our leaders.

If we see leadership as a skill that everyone can develop and improve through training and practice, I believe we will be approaching leadership in the right way. Only then can we take advantage of every individual's unique knowledge, experience, and personal traits. The gap between the expectations of what a leader ought to do, and what, in fact, a leader actually can do, will be smaller. And this brings us back to playing musical instruments. In most cases, talented musicians have taken lessons and have learned from someone who is better than they are and who has played the instrument for longer. The best musicians have practised incredibly hard. But don't they make mistakes at times? Of course they do. If we consider leadership to be a skill, we can understand that we have to learn from someone else, practise a great deal and increase our level of tolerance for making mistakes. A musician who makes a mistake is not a bad musician and a leader who makes mistakes is not a bad leader.

Indeed, tolerance for making mistakes is a prerequisite for being able to participate in certain activities, such as sports. Most elite athletes miss their target more often than hitting it. A high-jumper knocks down the bar more times than leaping over it. In baseball, the best batsmen miss the ball at least two-thirds of the time. If you transfer this reasoning to most organizations and leadership models, there is much less leeway for making mistakes.

Many years ago, I watched an interview with the then head of ABB, one of Sweden's top corporations, Percy Barnevik. The interviewer pointed out a major failure at ABB and asked Percy, in an accusatory tone, whether it was a mistake on his part. Barnevik replied, very calmly, acknowledging that he had made a mistake. When the reporter tried to make an issue of the incident, Barnevik simply said: "I make many mistakes. I make mistakes every day. In fact, making mistakes is part of my job." After getting that answer, the reporter was hard-pressed to expand on the question.

What happens if we don't dare to take risks? The fact of the matter is, we have to take risks, regardless of what we are working on. Managers and leaders have to take risks. A fundamental principle of business is that the higher the risk, the higher the return. In business, the proof that you are taking risks is that you make money. Another form of proof is that things sometimes fail miserably. A leader should be able to have bad days, make poor decisions, experience life crises and fall ill. The organizational and leadership models have to be able to survive it – as long as we have human leadership. If we wish to succeed in our activities, in the real world, we have to rely on leadership models that allow leaders to be normal people – and nothing more. Leadership is a skill, management is a role and people are always just people.

It was with great humility, even a little trepidation, that I allowed this book to be published. Every year, thousands of books about leadership are published and very few offer anything new; many provide nothing of value. Some readers may not feel this book offers much new information, other than the fact that the content is expressed in my own way, based on my own unique experiences. However, the aim of my book is mainly to make people think: people who are, or who want to be, leaders in an organization, and also people who are non-managers. If my book compels you to question your own views about leadership and management, then it has been of reasonable benefit. I will be happy if you do not agree with my ideas and conclusions once you've read the book, provided you have honestly questioned your own perceptions.

COMMANDMENT 1

Be humble: as a manager, you are also a team member.

Have you ever noticed that the higher up you rise in an organization's hierarchy, the smarter and more gifted you apparently become? This isn't because you have suddenly gained natural talents, it's down to how you are perceived by other people. Naturally, it's easy to get sucked into believing you are, in fact, the Oracle of Delphi. Many people expect you to have all the answers and to be ever available with sound advice. There is no question that it affects your self-perception. Your self-confidence will grow as, in your new elevated position, your opinions and ideas are warmly accepted, where once they would have been greeted with lukewarm enthusiasm, at best. Now your ideas are good, even brilliant. Whatever you say or suggest is met with a nod; open criticism disappeared the day you assumed your higher office. At this point, it is natural to become over-confident in your abilities.

As a manager and leader, you must remind yourself frequently that you are exactly the same as everyone else, neither better nor worse. If you were to gather a thousand managers together with a thousand of their team members and give them an intelligence test, I'd bet the managers' intelligence would prove to be roughly equal to that of their staff. It is also probable that many of the non-managers would have a higher level of intelligence than their managers. This may seem surprising, as many people expect those in higher positions to be much better and wiser, but that is an unreasonable fantasy, particularly in light of the fact that managers are recruited out of regular employees. If you agree with this line of reasoning, you may also agree that over-confidence in your own abilities is not an accurate picture of reality either. None of us is infallible. You have to understand that, as a manager and leader, you are going to be better at certain things than others, just like everyone else.

If there is something that distinguishes a leader – at least, a good leader – from other people, it is their social and emotional competence, not their intellectual gifts. A growing number of studies indicate that what is known as emotional intelligence (EQ), plays a greater role in professional success than does IQ. In a study by Spencer et al (1997), six emotional competencies were identified, which seemed to separate the most successful managers from the average ones. These were: influence; team leadership; organizational awareness; self-confidence; achievement drive; and leadership. Other studies show that exceptional managers can be up to 127% more productive than an average manager and more than 80% of this difference derives from EQ. (Hunter, Schmidt and Judiesch, 1990; Goleman, 1998).

To be fair, research on EQ has engendered some criticism, much of it aimed at how EQ is measured. Some people contend that it is a new way of packaging the same behavioral perspectives that we have long talked about. But most agree that these 'soft' human competences or important and have a major influence on the success of individuals and organizations. (Murphy, 2006).

A wise manager should take advantage of team members' strengths and compensate for their weaknesses, to ensure others feel confident to question decisions and offer comments and criticism.

Your job within the organization is to lead others, and not necessarily to come up with all the answers yourself. But as a manager, you may not always know which people around you are genuine and which are only pretending to agree with you. An arrogant manager, or a manager with too much ego, often surrounds himself with yes-men or 'brown-nosers', since the atmosphere he has created does not invite or even tolerate employees who question decisions or suggest solutions. Even in companies with a more open environment, you will find yes-men. The problem with these individuals is that they look like ordinary people and it can be difficult to identify them.

Another challenge around gaining a realistic view of your own competence as a leader has to do with people's attitudes towards power. We all tend to relate differently to people with power and influence, and that is not necessarily a good thing for a leader. Team members who respond negatively to authority figures may be difficult to tolerate.

Yes-men, on the other hand, have respect for power and a tendency to think that the manager is always right and is more knowledgeable than other team members. They do not question or criticize authority. In psychology, this is called a 'halo effect' (Thorndike, 1920). It means that, because we perceive a person to have certain strong and positive characteristics, we attribute other positive traits to him or her. For example, we may listen to a famous movie star or baseball player offering their opinions on child rearing and attribute greater validity to their opinions than we would someone else, simply because he or she is an excellent actor or athlete. By the same token, yes-men feel that people with power have that power for a reason. They must have gained power by being good at what they do and therefore they see no reason to doubt it.

A variation on the yes-man is the 'boot-licker' or sycophant. A certain amount of flattery and subordination is neither wrong nor abnormal. And most of us tell the odd 'white lie' to be kind or polite. I recall a debate between my mother, my father and I. My mother believed that you should always be honest, and for her, even white lies were not okay. My father and I felt that white lies could be fine, and in fact, 100% honesty could be mean and hurtful, in some situations.

For example, if someone came into work and excitedly asked, "what do you think of my new tie?" I might tell them it suited them, despite that not being a completely honest answer. My mother felt that if a person asked you what you thought, you should tell them – and perhaps prevent them from walking around wearing an ugly tie. Regardless of which side of this debate you are on, the everyday 'suck up' is just trying to be nice. The boot-licker is something different, sneakier and more calculating.

This person has figured out what they can gain from sucking up to a person in power, by agreeing with them and manipulating them. In fact, there are people who realize in advance that a manager's decisions or actions could lead to a minor catastrophe but remain silent because, in the long run, they know they may gain from the manager's mistake.

A manager's behavior can lead to yes-men, but it can also contribute to an atmosphere that makes it easier for team members to develop a more honest and realistic attitude towards the abilities and decisions of a manager. As leader, you have to be able to tell the difference between *actually* succeeding and only perceiving that you have succeeded when you have accomplished a task. If you truly want to achieve the goals of your organization, you need honest feedback and other people's viewpoints, and of course, you have to accept suggestions for improvement, including criticisms of you or the status quo. And that is not possible if you are surrounded by yes-men.

I had first-hand experience of a boot-licker shortly after becoming the head of the Swedish cell phone business for the largest phone company in Nordic countries, Telia. I was supposed to attend a quarterly meeting with our CEO. My manager and I arrived at the meeting a little early to prepare and he turned to me and said:

"Kelly, I know we have many problems in our company but in this meeting we will only talk about positive things." In other words, an executive vice-president was asking his senior vice-president to lie to the CEO. When the management team intentionally feeds the CEO half-truths and lies it becomes impossible for him or her to develop a reasonable understanding of the challenges facing the organization and will ultimately lead to failure for the CEO, the organization or both.

In other words, the climate a manager creates depends, in large part, on what a manager wants to achieve.

The yes-man attitude is not just the responsibility of the manager, even though it is the manager who cultivates a yes-man culture. It is up to each individual team member to decide whether they want to work in that kind of atmosphere. It is frightening to think that we learned somewhere not to criticize people with power and influence (at least, not to their faces), and that life is simpler and less complicated if we go with the flow and dodge every bump and pothole in the road. But think about the day you retire, look back on your life and realize that you never accomplished anything. You fooled yourself into thinking you achieved something, because you believed in the flattery from all the ingratiating people, and bathed in a glow of false accomplishment.

I believe that most of us want praise, which is understandable, but in an ideal world, we should only desire praise for something we have genuinely achieved. That is why I was a little worried when my ten-year-old son phoned me one afternoon and asked if he could skip his language lesson because he found it boring, and felt that he didn't learn anything from it anyway because it was too easy. (I should mention that, since I am an American living in Sweden, my children receive home-tutoring in English.) I asked my son whether he had tried to explain to his teacher how he felt about it.

"I can't," he replied quickly. "Teachers don't like hearing bad stuff like that."

"But if you talk politely to the teacher and explain that you think it is too easy, which makes it boring, maybe you can find a solution to the problem so that you learn more and enjoy it."

"No, I can't. The teacher will get angry and that's no fun."

So my ten-year-old son had already learned that life is easier if you can put up with a boring teacher and refrain from saying what you think. You just keep your mouth shut and pretend everything is fine (or skip classes and avoid the problem altogether). To avoid any hassle, he said nothing to his teacher. I tried to explain to him that if all students just nodded and said nothing, the teacher might be under the false impression that he or she was doing a good job.

> One way to avoid the yes-man is to admit there is a problem and point it out. It will not disappear on its own; you as the manager have to deal with it.

When I arrive as a new manager in a business, I usually encourage my employees to give me feedback and even offer criticism. I make it known that I want to hear their opinions. I also explain that I am only human, and that I don't always deal with criticism very well and can get nervous or defensive. That is not because I don't want to hear their criticism, but because it's simply how I sometimes react. I also point out that I don't hold grudges. I try to be honest about my own shortcomings as a manager. For instance, I might admit that I have a tendency to take over meetings and that it's ok to tell me to be quiet if I do that.

It is up to me to act on suggestions and demonstrate that suggestions or criticisms can actually lead to a change. In order to create the trust you need for this type of dialogue, you need to be humble. Showing your humility to others is one of the most important qualities a leader can have. You cannot be too proud to admit you have made a mistake. No-one is perfect. You should be proud of what you can do and what you achieve, but never believe you are infallible. You must anchor yourself in values that keep you grounded, when it might become easy to soar and give yourself too much credit. This is not something that is only typical of our time; in ancient Rome, people were aware of the importance of humility and the need to be reminded of it. Whenever a general won a great victory in the Roman Empire and paraded through the streets of Rome to the cheers and adulation of the crowds, a slave always stood behind them in the chariot whispering in his ear *"memento mori"* (remember you are mortal).

A manager can show his humility by asking questions and letting his staff make suggestions and come up with solutions. Instead of saying "we are facing a huge challenge and I think we should do this...", you could express it with a little humility: "We have a huge challenge to deal with. What do you think we should do?"

Being humble as a manager or a leader does not diminish your authority. In fact, it has the opposite effect. When you are humble and you start to take responsibility and can admit to making mistakes, you will go up in your employees' estimation and this will enhance your authority. This will also give others the courage to express what they really think, which in the long run, cuts down on the number of yes-men. It results in a positive chain reaction making for better decisions and achieving better results.

As a manager, I have often gravitated towards individuals who are honest and straightforward – almost blunt – in terms of commenting on my behavior and the behavior of others. I have made these types of people my closest advisors, even when my own manager has advised me to fire them or move them somewhere else because of their outspoken opinions. In each of these cases, I have defended the actions of the staff members in question, by explaining that they are only being honest and want the best for the company, so I need to listen to what they have to say.

For the sake of the business, managers sometimes have to accept scathing criticism.

There's another side to this. Although many managers have an overblown sense of self-confidence, there are those who wrestle with waning self-esteem. Some may battle to hide this with grandiose displays of arrogance and superiority, but the truth is that everyone feels inadequate at one time or another. Every good manager knows, deep down, that you cannot always live up to other people's expectations, no matter how much praise and admiration is lavished upon you by those around you. Your work may seem overwhelming and the feeling that you cannot handle the situations you face may keep growing inside you.

Once, I was working very intensively with a staff member who was due to take over from me. After about a month in his new position, he called me and said:

"Kelly, I cannot do this."

"Of course you can," I said, struggling to understand his doubt.

"No, this isn't working, because I am not like you."

I explained to him that no-one expected him to be like me, because I am a master of being me, and he is a master of being him. He shouldn't worry about what I used to do, or how I used to do it when I was in the same position. His job was not to try and duplicate my methods, or those of anyone else, for that matter. He had to find his own way of running the business and put his own personal stamp on the job.

Once he realized this, he took the company to much greater heights than I had ever succeeded in doing. But despite his success, he remained worried and uncertain, and inside, he had a sense that he just wasn't good enough. He used to wonder when he would be found out, when the rest of the world would realize he wasn't that good and didn't know as much as they thought he did. The fear of being exposed as inferior in a job is known as 'imposter syndrome'. Studies have shown that 40% of top executives have suffered from imposter feelings and a sense of inadequacy at some time in their careers. These people usually believe their success is only, or mostly, the result of external factors and not due to their own talents, skills and abilities. Many managers also feel their success is the result of pure coincidence and luck. It is not uncommon for managers with low self-esteem to have these types of feelings and thoughts.

In my introduction, I used the examples of George Washington and Abraham Lincoln to illustrate how external circumstances helped make them legends of US history. But this doesn't mean they weren't good leaders. I believe the circumstances at the time may have helped to eliminate other individuals who did not have the leadership abilities necessary to handle the difficult conditions that existed at the time. In fact, circumstances during the civil war were so difficult that Lincoln had to replace a number of his generals before he found a leader by the name of Grant, who finally succeeded in winning the war. The simple reality is that long-term success as a manager may well be the result of a combination of competence, circumstances, and even a little luck.

Managers suffering from imposter syndrome sometimes act in a way that makes it easier for others to see through them. The way they talk, coupled with tentative behavior and attempts to extricate themselves from difficult situations using gimmicks and circumvention, confuses staff members and does not contribute to clarifying the manager's goals and visions. By acting like this, there is a greater chance that a manager will be questioned, which for a manager with imposter syndrome would be a nightmare reinforcing their sense of inadequacy. Some managers adopt a 'know-it-all' attitude and every conversation or piece of feedback can, to them, expose their bluff. They prefer to surround themselves with yes-men.

I believe that all of us are (or should be) concerned about being inadequate, afraid that we cannot handle new situations and major challenges. It is only human to feel this way. But we cannot hide behind a false humility. We must acknowledge, and remind ourselves, that we have strengths, skills and talents. We also have our weaknesses and areas in which we struggle and need help.

Accept the help you need. Adopt a nuanced, mature approach and remember that although you are a manager, you are also a member of staff and an ordinary human being.

Tips to help you to be humble

1. Find a mentor with whom you can open up.
2. Be mindful of diversity: differing backgrounds, culture, gender and ages, anything to generate creative tension in the company.
3. Seek regular feedback from others. Listen to them, preferably without making comments about criticism to avoid growing defensive.
4. Encourage, thank and reward anyone who is honest with you, even if the truth hurts.

COMMANDMENT 2

Dare to delegate: your job
is to dare to lead others,
not to have all the answers.

This commandment begins with a summary: make sure your organization has the best people and listen to them. You cannot win alone!

To put it a little harshly, the day we begin to believe we have become managers because we are better than 'ordinary' employees is the day we will find ourselves skating on thin ice. If you or I have the notion that we are smarter or more gifted than other staff members, it is time for us to quit!

Any organization in which you believe you are the smartest person, will most certainly be hammered by its competitors. The strength of an organization is in its collective know-how, not in what each individual person believes or does. Psychological research shows that, when something good happens to a person, they believe it to be the result of their own ability (Buunk and van Yperen, 1991), but when something bad happens, it is down to external circumstances. At the same time, we tend to believe the opposite for other people. The bad things that happen to others are their own fault while the good things are due to external circumstances or luck (Ross, 1977). This can be a devastating attitude for anyone who wants to develop as a leader. To gain as true and impartial a view of reality as possible, we have to be aware of these tendencies, both within ourselves as leaders and in others.

If you are particularly skilled in a given area and no-one takes advantage of your abilities, it may be because you have a manager who doesn't listen, or in the worst case, a leader who thinks he or she is the best himself or herself. In order for your skills and abilities to come to the fore, the organization must be able to unleash an employee's abilities, so that their capabilities are exploited. A manager who understands that concept increases the company's chances of finding more successful solutions and achieving better results – which are the keys to success.

There is usually an explanation for a manager's incredible faith in his or her own prowess and abilities. Most of these individuals have been promoted to various positions of leadership because they were considered highly capable in their previous positions. If they then do well in their new roles, they may continue to be promoted over and again. It might not, then, seem so strange that people who land top executive positions begin to believe they are especially gifted and better than everyone else. Who is going to question them? And why would you listen to someone else when you already know you are the best?

In times during which we implement one reorganization after another in our eagerness to find the perfect organizational structure, we discover that, more often than not, there is nothing wrong with the structure. On the other hand, we rely on the wrong processes and are not sufficiently flexible in our dealings with the world around us and its constant evolution. In many cases, the type of organization we choose is often of lesser importance. The simplicity of the structure is important. A simple organization can be more flexible and easier to adapt without needing to restructure the entire organization.

When I was studying for my MBA at the Stockholm School of Economics, we had a professor named Gunnar Hedlund. He conducted research into how international businesses organize themselves. I admired him and listened studiously to what he had to say. One evening, the entire class went to a pub nearby and I got to sit beside Gunnar. I asked him whether the research had identified one organizational structure that was better than any other.

I had already worked for a few years, before starting at the School of Economics, so I had seen, first-hand, how large companies struggled with frequent reorganizations to try to find the right structure. In those days, matrix organizations were all the rage, in which everyone had two or three managers. During my time at the Whirlpool Corporation, I remember we discussed three-dimensional matrices. I wondered whether Gunnar could give me a few insights, based on his research, as to whether the matrix was the right solution, whether we should return to the traditional hierarchical organization, or whether there was, in fact, another solution we should be considering.

I took to heart what he told me. Laughing, he replied that, according to his research, the type of organization had no bearing on success at all. He said that companies reorganize to try to adapt to changes around them, but that the world around them changes much faster than they can reorganize. It becomes a race in which the reorganized company always comes second.

His recommendation was to choose a simple organizational structure and to maintain it over a long period of time. He suggested that I should invest my resources and energy in teaching the organization to be flexible and adaptable in its processes.

I have also observed, in my professional life, that although reorganizations demand a great deal of resources and involvement from everyone concerned, they seldom result in actual improvement. I have also experienced how a lack of interest, for a number of reasons, combined with a manager's unwillingness to listen, have cost companies and employees more than you can put a price on. No company will improve when employees become disengaged, and just shrug their shoulders in resignation when faced with an organizational restructure that resembles a change introduced relatively recently... without much in the way of improvement.

The famous quote by Charlton Ogburn Jnr (1911-1998) in *Harpers* magazine in January 1957 (often falsely attributed to Roman satirist Gaius Petronius Arbiter) sums it up well. "We trained hard, but it seemed that every time we were beginning to form up into teams, we would be reorganized. I was to learn later in life that we tend to meet any new situation by reorganizing; and a wonderful method it can be for creating the illusion of progress while producing confusion, inefficiency, and demoralization."

I have been involved in several radical reorganizations over the years, one of which was when I worked at TeliaSonera. They reorganized the company fairly often, roughly once every 18 months, sometimes more often. Each time it was done, it was to ensure the company would be able to cope with the latest demands from the business environment. No sooner were we beginning to feel at home within the new structure, then it was time for another reorganization. Naturally, this triggered questions and concern among the employees and many of them wondered why the new organization would be better than the old one.

It was always introduced to cope with new demands but it didn't take long before it was discovered that it wasn't good enough. It became a little tragi-comic each time the top executives had to stand up and tell us that this next reorganization was designed to help us get closer to our customers (just as the last four reorganizations had been). I asked our HR manager how a reorganization would bring us closer to our clients, when in fact there would be no more of us working in sales or customer service (often, there ended up being fewer employees). The truth of the matter was that, at best, management simply believed (or hoped) they could lower costs; at worst they had no clue as to what the actual benefits of a reorganization would be. Why should we believe this new organization would not need reorganizing all over again?

This was a good question. And no-one knew the answer... until afterwards. But I have seldom heard upper-level executives taking responsibility and admitting they did not know how things would turn out, that they were wrong and that they did not understand the consequences. However, they cannot know everything, and they definitely cannot predict the future.

Within TeliaSonera, we were either organized according to sectors of technology (mobile telephones, landlines, broadband) or by customer type (consumer, small- and medium-sized enterprise, large corporate). When we were organized by technology, we discovered several sub-optimizations, such as when a customer wanted to purchase services from us in both the mobile and landline sectors. It was difficult for us to treat them as one customer and generate a single invoice for the customer's entire purchase. It was also a challenge for one person within customer service to gain an overview of the customer's entire involvement with us. There was no real incentive for a manager at Telia Mobile, for instance, to invest in a system to help his colleagues at Telia Landline to resolve the invoicing problem they shared. So, instead, we reorganized according to customer type, to enable us to focus, in a holistic way, on the entire customer within one organizational unit.

But then other sub-optimizations arose, with each organization wanting to develop its own consumer or company services, independently, although the services were basically the same. This pushed up development costs, and to handle it, we reorganized again, reverting to being organized by technology sector.

I brought this up at a meeting and suggested that the problems didn't necessarily relate to our organizational structure. The problem was perhaps that, regardless of how we were organized, we had to learn to work across the whole organization, despite differing department affiliations. Had our managers listened more closely to the voices within the organization they would have realized that the major problem was a lack of cooperation between various organizational units, which were not listening to one another's needs. That poor communication was mainly the result of bad leadership by managers within the different technology and business sectors.

There is nothing to indicate that a person who is highly competent within a specific work area will make a good manager or leader. Once, when I was speaking at a conference for sales managers, I asked for a show of hands from anyone who had been the best salesperson before being promoted to sales manager. About 90% raised their hands.

While it's untrue to say the best salespeople cannot be good sales managers, the chances are equally high that a mediocre salesman could make a good sales manager.

The qualities that make a good leader are not the same as those needed to be a good salesman. If a good salesman fails to become a good sales manager, the business has gained a poor manager and lost an effective salesperson, which is costly.

Doctors often have more difficulty accepting a hospital director who is not a clinician over one who is, although the skills needed to run a hospital are not the same as those required to treat patients. The skill-sets required to run a development department are not the same as those needed by the engineers who work in that department. Leading the department requires different abilities to the ones integral to product development or writing new program code. And yet we act as though expertise in sales or engineering, for instance, qualifies someone to be a manager or leader.

As I explained earlier, leadership is a skill, just like any other. Being a talented musician does not necessarily mean you are a good athlete. These are two totally different skill-sets. Being an excellent salesman, doctor or development engineer, does not equate to being an effective manager or leader.

Some years ago, I went from being a marketing manager with Whirlpool Corporation to becoming president of Whirlpool's Swedish subsidiary. I started the Swedish operation from scratch and hired our entire staff, which included the new marketing manager. Looking back, I can only say that he did not have an easy time of it. I had trouble keeping my nose out of his work and gladly offered my views on pretty much anything and everything he did. I thought I could do his job even better than he was doing it, so I meddled in everything. As a result, he never felt satisfied with his own work. He must have thought I was an absolute pain. It took time for me to realize that he was doing the job his way, and it was no worse for that. Of course, it was tough to keep quiet when I thought my way was better. So one day, the marketing manager came into my office and said:

"Kelly, you are an excellent marketing manager. But I wonder who is doing your job while you are doing mine?"

I took his point.

When I look back on those days, I don't think I was the better marketing manager. But even had I been marginally better, would that have made it acceptable for me to neglect the entire strategic management of the company? Definitely not. Had I felt that the marketing manager was not good enough at his job, I should have replaced him, not done the job for him. I was not appointed president to be an expert on all the specific skills needed in our business, I was hired to lead the company.

In the case of the marketing manager, I had two choices: I could help him develop and ensure he grew into his role, or go out and find someone who could do the job better. My job was to make sure my team members knew their jobs. I lacked the skills to do everyone's jobs for them, and it would have been suboptimal for me to sacrifice my own job in order to compensate for other people who were underperforming.

A few years later, I became head of Telia Mobile in Sweden, the cell phone division of Sweden's leading telecommunications company, and I went through the same thing again. Truth be told, I was a little intimidated when I took up the position. I had never been head of such a large operation and the people in the management group were indeed experts in each of their respective sectors: technology, legal, HR, finance and so on. There was no-one in the management group who wasn't more knowledgeable than me in their own area of expertise. It didn't take me long to realize that they didn't need a boss to help them with technology problems or to discuss legal issues. They needed a leader.

In an ideal world, the manager should have a good general understanding of the entire operation, but his or her specialist competence is always to lead. One way for a manager to develop an understanding of the company is to listen and learn. In a group discussion, you don't always need to be the person who speaks first. If you have a strong opinion about something, you shouldn't withhold it. But if you explain what you think right away, it can colour the entire debate and there is a good chance that the discussion will revolve around your opinion as manager and not what the employees think. This results in them listening to you and not the other way around. The key is to open up so that others dare to say what they think. Sit quietly, listen, and process their ideas. Demonstrate that you have taken what they are saying into consideration.

Another option is to delegate an entire issue and ask the group to come up with suggestions and solutions. Then consider what the group has come up with before making a decision, because, as manager, you cannot succeed alone. In fact, I would go so far as to say that you, as a good leader, don't even have to make any decisions. You just have to make sure that decisions are made. You can delegate decision-making, provided you trust in your staff. If you don't, you have a problem, either with yourself or with your staff. But if you have confidence in your people, you can trust them to make the right decisions; no doubt better than the decisions you would have made on your own. You are there to lead, not to know everything.

Tips to help you delegate

1. Set aside time and resources to develop your own leadership skills using training and personal reflection.
2. Let employees take responsibility for their work.
3. Stay quiet more often.
4. Gain greater leverage from your leadership by working through others rather than doing the work yourself.

COMMANDMENT 3

Maintain your freedom: never get yourself into a situation where you cannot afford to tell the company to go to hell.

What happens when you become a manager? Besides gaining authority and responsibility, you are usually paid more. Most of us spend that extra money relatively quickly. Perhaps you are promoted again and receive an even bigger pay rise. Even that extra money will find its way into your overall consumption and soon you won't even notice you've had a salary increase.

After a while, you may well discover you've adapted to a lifestyle that you would struggle to give up, although it is costing you a great deal. Your work may not seem as fascinating as it once did and has become something you feel forced to do rather than something you want to do. Mondays are not the start of a stimulating working week but the beginning of a tedious working week. More often than not, you think about doing something different. But what happens with the debts you have accumulated based on your current salary, such as your mortgage, cars, your boat, on instalment payments – and to your ability to make impulse purchases?

Everything you have today, which looks great on the face of it, can put you in a situation where you have difficulty moving forward. Instead, you find yourself in one spot, treading water. But a new job might be exactly what you need to feel better and to provide an outlet for your creativity and ambitions – even if it does not pay as well as your current role.

My father found himself in this type of situation. At one point he had a job he really liked, but a boss who made his life almost unbearable. When I suggested he change jobs, he replied quickly:

"Sure, I could do that! I could find a new job any day I wanted for half the pay."

If we get a better job and a couple of thousand more in salary, it won't take long before we've spent that extra income on something that drives up our expenses or obligations. The money that could act as a little extra padding, giving us greater freedom, goes on yet more consumption, a nicer car with pricier insurance;

a holiday home, with all the extra expenses that entails and the obligation to holiday there every year.

You stay in your job because you have to and have been hit by the *fear factor* ('prostitution factor' as one of my friends calls it). This is the fear of taking a stand and risking becoming an undesirable at work, or saying something that could cause you to lose your job; it quickly kills any entrepreneurial spirit or motivation. You end up in a golden cage. The cage may be pleasant, even luxurious, but it's still a cage.

I often speak at secondary schools and one of the most common questions from students is "what do you think I should study at college?" It's an odd question to ask a stranger. How can I tell a young person I've never met before what he or she should study? At the same time, it's indicative of the wonderfully unfettered attitude you hope to see in young people. The feeling that they can be anything they want to be. All they have to do is choose!

Many of the young people I talk to are interested in a job that pays well. My advice to these students is to forget about money and instead find work they enjoy. I always suggest they study something they like and are interested in, no matter what it is. You have to enjoy what you are doing to be able to invest the time and energy needed to be good at it. If you are good at what you do, it will be profitable for you, and even more importantly, you will enjoy your work and gain personal satisfaction from it.

I usually tell young people that they can expect to work for 40 to 50 years, and choosing a job they don't like just to achieve a high salary is like choosing a prison – albeit with silk sheets.

When I was around 30 years old, I was working at Whirlpool Corporation's European headquarters in northern Italy. At the time, I was a commercial product manager for Whirlpool's microwave oven business in Europe. While I was working there, I got to know a man who became my mentor. He was a senior executive in Whirlpool's European organization and I respected him a great deal, but he was not directly involved in the business area in which I was working. This made for an excellent mentor relationship. He was extremely knowledgeable about our business environment and company, but had no direct influence over me or my work.

One night, after we had been working late, we chatted for a while and he advised me: "Never get yourself into an economic situation where you can't afford to tell the company to go to hell!" This ethos doesn't mean you have to feel animosity towards your employer. On the contrary! The most loyal thing you can do is to create conditions within which you always have your back covered, so you can say what you think and dare to take risks. You may not hold the same view as other people in the company, but that doesn't mean there is something wrong with you, or the company; in fact, it can help build a positive dynamic.

My mentor explained that, if you are sitting in that golden cage, two things are likely to happen: first and foremost, there is an enormous risk that you will lose your sense of job satisfaction. Second, your value to the company will diminish. When you find yourself in a situation where you have become financially reliant on your current job and have sacrificed your independence, you will probably stop taking chances and saying what you think, particularly if this would be uncomfortable for your superiors.

The paradox is that the less dependent you are on the company, the greater the chance that you will create something of value for it. While you are still financially independent and dare to speak your mind, even when doing so feels inconvenient and uncomfortable, you will be enriching the company. The day you become a bobblehead doll who nods "yes" to everything, and you feel that you have to suppress your views, is the day you lose much of your motivation and drive. You are then working because you have to and not because you want to.

It can be tempting for a manager to try to bind a team member to an organization, through indirect and/or direct pressure. I remember one manager at my first job after I finished college. He nagged me all the time, encouraging me to buy a house, or at least an expensive car. I started to wonder why he was so interested, and one day I asked him. He looked me in the eyes and said bluntly: "If you get into debt, there is a much greater chance that you will stay in this job."

Although, I didn't take on any major debt while I was working there, my manager may have been telling the truth. Maybe I would have stayed longer had I been deeper in debt and become financially dependent on the company, but I am not as convinced it would have been the best solution for the company or for my manager. By increasing my dependence, my productivity may have fallen, along with my job satisfaction. Then there would have been no winners, only losers.

Your freedom is not based on how much you consume. You cannot buy motivation or job satisfaction. Freedom means making your own decisions about your life and being responsible for the consequences.

The freedom to decide for yourself whether you want to stay in a job, or leave for pastures new, comes from not being financially dependent on it, regardless of your salary. Free will is a key component in all successful relationships. Who wants to be in a romantic relationship with a partner who doesn't really want to be with you but stays because they like the lifestyle? That would be an unhealthy relationship. The same can be said of a work relationship in which one of the partners doesn't want to continue but cannot afford to change the situation. You are the one who creates your own 'golden cage', and it is you who creates your own freedom.

Other factors can also trap you in a job, including status. When I was working for Whirlpool, the company conducted a revision of all employees' job titles. Titles had been inflated to the point where it was almost impossible to understand what roles individuals actually had. Everyone relatively senior had vice president or director titles. The result of this title revision was that everyone kept their jobs and benefits, but many vice presidents became ordinary directors and many of the directors became managers. Lots of people were upset by this and some were so disappointed they actually left the company, despite nothing having changed in terms of their roles or salaries. These people seemed to define their identities and self-worth by their titles. When their titles were downgraded, they felt their value within the company, the job market and possibly even as human beings had been reduced as well.

The opposite can also be true. I have seen people stay in jobs they weren't enjoying because of a grand job title. I was on the board of a company owned by my then employer, TeliaSonera. This was a small technology company with about 15 employees, and it was extremely generous with titles, which is not unusual in small, start-up technology companies. It had a fairly young staff and everyone had titles such as CEO, chief financial officer (CFO), chief technology officer (CTO) and chief information officer (CIO).

At one point, I sat and talked with the CEO of the company and he told me that he had a couple of employees who were tired of their jobs and didn't really want to stay on. He perceived it as a problem, because they had difficulty finding new jobs. I didn't see it as a problem. These employees were well-educated and should have been in demand within the job market. Moreover, their present salaries were not particularly high. He agreed with me that these employees should be able to find work fairly quickly, with better pay, but that they would find it difficult to find job titles such as CFO, CTO or CIO. According to him, they understood that they had never been chief officers in the true sense of the title, but that they were so accustomed to their titles and status, they baulked at the idea of losing them.

Geographic location can also bind people to their jobs. A person might live somewhere because he or she likes it there, even though they don't like their job. Even if that person wants to change jobs, the number of jobs available locally may be limited, so he or she will stay put in order to stay in their current home.

To conclude this commandment, ask yourself why it is necessary to pay a manager a higher salary than he or she received previously. The reason is that a manager has to be a risk taker and the higher salary is, frankly, a form of risk premium. If you accept the position of manager with a risk premium, part of the job is to take more risks. If you take the risk premium, then you have to take risks. This is unavoidable.

Tips to help you maintain your freedom

1. Save a little money so you always have financial leeway.
2. Negotiate a longer period of notice or severance pay with your employer.
3. Think long term. Focus on relationships and purposes more than on rewards or benefits (this will actually increase your chances of gaining rewards).

COMMANDMENT 4

Take Risks: Losing your job is not the worst think that can happen, it is often the best thing.

Many people think the worst that could happen to them in their career would be to get fired, especially if they were to lose their job because of something they did wrong. The potential sense of failure, the embarrassment and the financial insecurity, tend to limit our willingness, and even our ability, to be creative and take risks. But all creativity involves risk, and without creativity, there is no growth or development, either in individuals, or in organizations. Consider, then, that there are managers whose main professional goal in life is to simply to keep their jobs; that there are people employed to lead others whose main objective is not being fired. Imagine how frustrating it must be to work under those conditions – both for the manager and his or her staff.

Far too many organizations, and their staff, are afraid to take risks. By choosing the safe path, a person could well stay in their job for 20 or 30 years, running the risk of stagnating in terms of their own personal growth and career opportunities. This can be far worse than losing your job. If you take no risks, you will gain no rewards.

We do things, make judgment calls and take risks that we hope will end well. Sometimes, the outcome is not precisely what we had planned, occasionally things end in disaster. But if you never experience a disaster, you have not taken any risks and have not reached out to grow. The key to building value and success in a company is daring to take risks.

I usually state the purpose of a company along the following lines:

"An enterprise is where people consume resources in processes to achieve results which create value for people."

If you take a closer look, you will see that the purpose of any organization is to create value for people. All those employed by an organization gain security through the salaries they earn and the work provides intellectual stimulation, social belonging and status. But a healthy organization cannot exist only to create value for its staff. It creates value for other people as well, including customers, shareholders, or tax payers. You could say that the ultimate goal of a company, of any organization for that matter, is to create value for people in society as a whole.

Generic value creation process

People use resources in processes to generate results that create value for people.

The concept of risk is fundamental in the world of business. Business schools all over the world teach their students that the higher the risk, the higher the return. Risk basically refers to the possibility that something may turn out different than expected. If an investment, for example, has a high risk of not living up to expectations then the potential return on that investment should also be higher, otherwise there would be no incentive for taking the greater risk.

I would argue that the risk and return concept is valid in all organizations whether they are businesses or not. As a society, we invest tax money in schools, infrastructure and healthcare because we believe we get greater value from our money than if we failed to invest in these services. Public sector workers and government agencies make decisions every day about how best to use the resources available to them, in order to create the best possible outcomes for citizens. A utilitarian such as John Stuart Mill might say that all human endeavour is a question of creating the greatest possible good with the least investment, or lowest cost (Utalitarianism, 1863). Sometimes, if the main objective of an organization is to create value by taking risks, then each individual must take risks too. It makes no difference what type of organization is involved, nor does its size or direction have any bearing; the same principles apply to its employees. If you understand these principles, you have understood your role in the process: to contribute to the company's value and development by taking risks.

The meaning of an individual's job is for them to determine for themselves. For some, it is the ability to support themselves, to have the security of knowing that their pay will arrive in their bank account every month. For others, simply supporting themselves is not enough and they strive to get a little more out of their jobs. Some people want to grow and develop and feel that their jobs are interesting and stimulating.

I am of the opinion that a 'healthy' company should encourage people to take risks. Nevertheless, more often than not, I hear people in business saying things such as "we need to minimize risk" and even "we must eliminate risk". When I have argued that we should encourage risk taking in companies, I have seen many managers look panicky, and I can almost hear them thinking: "What if an employee takes a risk that costs us a fortune, or even worse, pushes us into bankruptcy?"

Indirectly, these managers see their own jobs being threatened. But there is a big difference between taking risks and making stupid mistakes. Taking a risk is not synonymous with playing Russian roulette and carelessly wasting resources by making wild guesses. Risk taking should be the result of a well-considered, fact-based decision, based on our abilities and expertise, while pushing the boundaries of our capabilities. Companies and organizations will fail in the long term if they cannot develop a culture that encourages risk taking.

The same goes for employees and their individual careers. The greater your responsibilities in a company, the greater the risks you must be willing to take. At least, that is what we should expect, but unfortunately the reality is frequently the opposite. In other words, the more power a person has or the more money they earn, the less prone they will be to risk taking. One explanation is that there are substantially more US$50,000-a-year jobs available than there are US$2m-a-year jobs. Looking at it this way, it is not so difficult to understand that someone with a salary of $2m might do everything in his or her power to keep the job, and so is tempted to avoid anything that could jeopardize their position.

The real problem is not that you can lose your job if you take risks – although that can happen – but that all too many companies, consciously or unconsciously, create a culture that inhibits risk taking. As a result, employees who want to achieve great results are forced to take unreasonably high personal risks in order to do something that may benefit the company. This, in turn, results in fewer and fewer people daring to make tough decisions.

By this, I mean an employee is faced with a tough decision when they see what is needed to help the company develop, but realize that the necessary steps are risky. Employees can choose to take the necessary steps and accept that they may be considered responsible for the failure if something goes wrong. Or they can choose not to take the risk and to live with the fact that, knowingly, they have failed to do what is best for the company. There is a big difference between not doing anything wrong and doing the right thing. In this era of aggressive focus on governance and compliance, it can be much easier just to do what you are told to do than to innovate. The old adage that "it takes 14 'yeses' to get a decision approved but only one 'no' to kill it", is truer than ever. The control mechanisms in many organizations are so rigorous that they inadvertently discourage innovation.

There are two fundamental conditions necessary for the creation of cultures in which risk taking is encouraged. The first one involves how you communicate within a company or organization. What distinguishes an environment open to risk taking is the fact that the company enables everyone to talk with one another. This may seem obvious, but in many organizations, you cannot disrupt the internal communications hierarchy.

In an ideal world, if a customer service staff member needed to talk to someone in group management, that person would be able to do so without having to question whether or not it was the right thing to do. Ask yourself how often such a need arises and it probably isn't that often. The point is that it shouldn't feel uncomfortable or risky for customer service staff to contact group management. It definitely shouldn't feel wrong, or engender a fear of the internal communications hierarchy. Unfortunately, this hierarchy is often so rigid that it is difficult, even for people who work closely with one another, to communicate effectively.

When I was vice president for group marketing at TeliaSonera I reported to a member of the executive management team. His manager was our CEO. It was quite common for the CEO to call me, or to drop by my workplace to discuss something. This was frustrating for my immediate manager who didn't appreciate the CEO bypassing him to talk directly to me. In fact, on one occasion, my manager came right out and said that he didn't want me speaking directly to the CEO. I only had one manager between me and the CEO. The CEO and I worked in the same office and often sat in the same meetings together... but my manager preferred me not talk to the CEO. I even asked my manager what I should do if the CEO walked over to my desk and asked me a question. When these kinds of conditions exist at the highest management levels in a company, how likely is it that somebody who has four or five managers between him and the person he needs to talk to, dares to do so?

The second condition involves how people perceive risk. A risk taker must not be viewed as a failure and treated like a pariah if things go wrong; failed initiatives should not be swept under the rug. All organizations and the individuals within them make mistakes, no matter how skilled or careful they might be. The question is how to deal with mistakes. If you pretend that they never happen or try to hide them, the mistakes will be of no value to you. You will be doomed to repeat the same mistakes over and over again. But by learning from them and studying what went wrong, mistakes can become an educational tool, and you learn not to repeat them.

A company that wants to develop profitability should establish a creative work climate, and not just encourage, but reward, risk takers. It shows that you trust your employees, wish to invest in their abilities and believe in their skills and expertise.

When I was working at Whirlpool's European headquarters in Italy, my manager asked me if I would like to head up a project. To his surprise, my answer was a flat "no". He responded that he had thought me to be an ambitious and driven young man who wanted to try almost everything, and so was surprised by my answer. But I had watched other people try to run the project in question and neither the project, nor the project group, had done well. I didn't want to take that kind of risk with my career. After I explained my reasoning, he looked at me and said: "I know we have done a poor job of supporting employees who have taken risks on behalf of the company. But if you take on this project and it does not succeed as we expected, I promise to back you completely."

I had so much faith in him that I assumed the reins for the project and got started. In the end, I too failed at this project. My manager asked me to put together a presentation to report what we had learned from the initiative and its setbacks, and what we should consider the next time we tackled it.

The day came for me to make my presentation. I walked into an auditorium filled with around 100 people. They were all senior managers, higher up in the corporate hierarchy than I was. I was not particularly happy about standing there in front of this audience of superiors, explaining my failures. Just before I was about to speak, my manager came up on stage.

"Before Kelly starts his presentation, I would like to say that we are well aware that this project is tough. It has been a challenge, but we also know it is important to us. We may well not have achieved the results we were hoping for, but I believe that, thanks to the work of Kelly and his project team, we are much closer to finding a solution than we ever have been. So, to show our appreciation of the hard work that went into the project I would like to present a travel voucher worth $1,000 to every member of the team."

So we each received a travel voucher, I made my presentation and we had serious discussions about how to move forward with the project. This showed that the company was open to failure and that it was willing to learn from mistakes. It was a very professional way to accept failure and reward effort, and it showed that it was ok to take risks. The people who worked on the project even received an extra bonus.

To create a risk-prone organization, you need open dialogue, without an obstructive communication hierarchy, and you also have to demonstrate, as a company, that you do allow failure and will even celebrate and reward it. Finally, you must empower your employees. By empowering employees, I mean the organization should give team members the opportunity to act and make decisions, and use their own personal judgment within the framework of their job. But a substantial number of companies suppress risk taking through constricting regulations, which also causes bottlenecks in the organization. That can feel highly repressive for employees and it is far from empowering for the people working in the organization. Nevertheless, you as a manager can, at times, encourage your staff to take risks, even though the environment does not encourage it.

I discovered this for myself when I was in charge of sales at Volvo Cars in Sweden. Ford owned Volvo at the time and had a strict, bureaucratic set of rules. Since I was in charge of sales, I had the right to make decisions up to about $2m. I had a number of regional managers under me, responsible for hundreds of millions of dollars in sales each, but they did not have the authority to decide on one single dollar of expenditure. A regional sales manager visiting a dealer to discuss promotions, for instance, was not authorized to make decisions that cost money. According to the company rulebook, he was forced to bring me into the picture, and then I would make a decision on the proposal. This was an enormous handicap that forced regional managers to track me down, while I had to try to stay as accessible as possible. But I was often in meetings or travelling and thus I became a human bottleneck. So I said to my regional managers: "You have the right to make decisions within the framework of my decision-making authority of $2m."

In reality, decisions of that magnitude were seldom required, but it was the easiest way to eliminate the bottleneck and make work easier for the regional managers. It wasn't long before the finance department got in touch with me, stating that I had circumvented the rules. Naturally, I disagreed. The company had given me the authority to make decisions up to $2m and so I made an 'executive decision' that enabled the regional managers to make decisions within my authoritative framework. By doing this, I took a risk and created a greater risk-taking tendency. But this also gave the regional managers the freedom to act in an environment that did not encourage risk taking.

Another significant advantage of delegating business decisions further down the organization is that, by doing so, you spread the business risk. In my example from Volvo, I could make decisions of up to $2m. This meant that I could also make a wrong decision that potentially cost the company $2m. Suppose my regional managers had been allowed to make decisions of, say, $200,000 each, in their daily work. This would mean they could only make bad decisions worth up to $200,000 as well.

Five regional managers would have to make two very poor decisions each in order to reach the same economic loss that I could achieve with just one decision. Even if you were to argue that the quality of the manager's decisions should be higher than that of their staff, it would be hard to argue that it would be ten times better. In reality, the quality of my regional manager's decisions might, in fact, have been better than mine since they often had a better knowledge of the details of a particular investment. Looking back, I don't recall ever having made any $2m decisions without kicking it around with my superiors and key colleagues. The fact that I have the right to make a decision of that level doesn't mean that I shouldn't seek advice from others, or even that I have to make the decision on my own.

A manager's job is not so much to make good decisions as it is to make sure that good decisions get made.

I have discovered that if I really want to ensure the quality of the decisions in my organization, I shouldn't always be the one making those decisions. As the leader of the organization, I am ultimately responsible for the consequences of the decision, but that doesn't mean I have to make it.

All companies are run by a combination of values and rules. I have often said that rules are made to help us, and when they do not help us, we should ignore them. This does not mean to say that you should not follow the rules that exist, but that it is important to remember that a company's rules are designed only to help create value in the company. If a rule doesn't contribute to creating the value you want to attain, you can make exceptions to that rule.

If a rule regularly causes conflicts with the value-creating processes, then you have to change it.

Time and again, I have seen people choose rules over the values. When I was at TeliaSonera, a customer who was an owner and president of a manufacturing company called me. He told me his company had been a client of Telia's for 30 years and that he purchased services for millions of dollars every year. He was extremely upset because, while moving their head office, his company had accidentally paid an invoice a month late, which resulted in a late payment fee of $20. He said that if we insisted on him paying the fee, he would switch suppliers.

I listened while he read from his notes, rattling off the names of all the people at TeliaSonera with whom he had spoken before ending up with me. I promised to credit him the $20 and also to give him an extra $100 dollars in compensation, but I also wanted a copy of the list of people he had spoken to. His list contained the names of ten different people in the company. I contacted each of them and they all gave me more or less the same answer. They said that they realized $20 was a negligible amount of money in this situation, but that "rules are made to be followed and what would happen if we just ignored all the rules?" That's when I launched into my sermon: "Rules only exist to help us, and when the rules come into conflict with one of our core values, such as customer service, then you have to bend the rules in keeping with the company's values."

I have also been in situations where managers and leaders have thought more about themselves than about the company. I have been in meetings where everyone has agreed that a particular plan of action would be best for the company but that it couldn't be implemented because it was not in line with the objectives of certain managers' balanced score cards – which, for them, meant lower bonus payouts.

Sometimes, managers think primarily about their own gain, even if it is at the cost of the company. This also sends out signals that the company has adopted a risk-averse culture, where rules replace values instead of supporting them. If you apply that same culture to a sports team, that team will never win a game. Michael Jordan said this about taking risks: "I've missed more than 9,000 shots in my career. I've lost almost 300 games; 26 times, I've been trusted to take the game winning shot and missed. I've failed over and over and over again in my life. And that is why I succeed."

Imagine a quarterback who didn't dare to take risks? How many passes would he complete? Not many. An artist who always sticks to the rules will never create a masterpiece. The principle is the same when it comes to a company.

If we think back to the point about being fired, there are very few people who actually lose their jobs as a result of risk taking. An employee's termination is often the result of other things. In my professional life, I have seen thousands of people lose their jobs in mass layoffs when companies have tried to lower their costs, but only on a couple of occasions have I seen people forced out of their jobs for saying what they think or taking risks. I usually kid around by saying that if you say what you think you will either be promoted or become a union representative, and either situation can be pretty attractive. But should you find yourself in a situation where you do lose your job, accept the fact that it was time to look elsewhere, rather than to stay with an employer who does not appreciate an employee's creativity and innovation. In the long run, this would inhibit your personal growth and you would not be as driven or as successful as you could have been.

So losing your job is not the worst thing that could happen. Definitely not. In fact, it may even be what is needed to propel you forward and ultimately the best thing that ever happened to you professionally.

Tips to help you create a culture of risk

1. Take calculated risks (throw a few more passes).
2. Make sure the objective of the organization is not to follow rules blindly. The rules are there to support the objectives of the organization and support its core values.
3. Encourage others to take risks.
4. Celebrate any failures.
5. Create conditions throughout the organization to learn from failure.

COMMANDMENT 5

Deliver actual results:
don't worry about company
politics; in the long run,
it's results that count.

ll forms of organization have company politics. By
this, I don't mean party politics; I mean the politics
that spring up within a group of people trying to
work together to achieve goals – hopefully common
goals. This is about the organization's policy and culture, how we
deploy resources and how decisions are made. Company politics
have to do with guidelines for how to act and which procedures
and processes to use when making important decisions; how we
cooperate; and, in particular, on how authority/power should be
divided up.

This type of pattern of action takes place in any group that is
formed, and it is only natural. In a company, politics mainly com-
prises organizational, financial, and administrative mechanisms,
all of which are conditions that ensure the organization achieves
its stated goals. The organizational mechanisms involve having the
right human resources to perform the work of the company while
the financial mechanisms ensure financial resources are available
to fund the company's activities and to assume profit and loss
responsibility for parts or all of the organization. The administrative mechanisms decide how budget is to be distributed, which
policies and strategies will be chosen, and how to produce the
information needed for important decisions. In large organizations, it is frequently personnel who run the administrative mechanisms. Through their advisory and support role for managers,
they can also exert an indirect control over them.

Another vital administrative mechanism is control of systems,
and in particular, which IT systems the company uses. IT departments have assumed more and more power, both directly and
indirectly, over the operative line operation in many organizations.

Remember that the three political mechanisms (organizational, financial, and administrative) exist for a single reason: to support the organization in its pursuit of creating value.

Even though the political mechanisms exist to enable the creation of value in the company, individuals or groups can abuse them for their own purposes. For instance, a manager may abuse the organizational mechanisms for the purpose of usurping more and more of the organization, and to gather departments under his or her control. Some bosses are intent on having a large number of employees reporting to them, as it is still quite common for an executive's salary and status to be determined based on the number of people they manage.

In today's modern organizations there are many new types of executive position which have enormous influence over organizations but involve few direct reports. Nonetheless, there are still quite a number of managers who prefer having 2,000 subordinates over 200 or 20.

The financial mechanisms may be abused by people with a personal goal to be responsible for as large a portion of the company's financial resources as possible. In addition to the perceived prestige that accompanies financial responsibility, rewards are often allocated based on the level of sales achieved or level of financial responsibility.

Sometimes, the objective of a group, or an individual, is to acquire or retain power, rather than achieving the set objectives of the company. That is when bad politics enter into things and the mechanisms in place are abused. They have either forgotten why they are there or they no longer care whether the company continues to exist and thrive, about the role it plays in society or the value it creates.

To avoid this situation, leaders must constantly communicate the purpose and aims of the company to staff members so they understand how they can contribute to achieving the goals that have been set. However, there is a tendency to 'under communicate' vital pieces of information because, to senior executives, the information is so obvious. Messages must be repeated again and again until they become the core message conveyed in every form of communication and meeting. It is equally important to clarify that goals themselves should not be used as tools for maintaining power or for gaining more power.

The political machinations of a workplace can manifest themselves in various ways. There is almost always one person who is liked by many executives, but that is not to say that this person is popular among other members of staff. This individual seems to have a great network of contacts and is always in the limelight, despite never seeming to achieve solid results.

I have witnessed such people standing up on stage at corporate functions, accepting praise and honours for successes everyone knows is the result of other people's inspiration and hard work. I have also encountered people, usually managers, who steadfastly dismiss an idea and do nothing to develop or support those who have submitted the proposal until the suggestion has gained widespread support and grown into a huge success. At this point, they jump on board and accept praise for the successful concept. This undermines the satisfaction and motivation of those who actually contributed to the success.

I have been in meetings where decisions are made, more or less openly, which do not benefit the company but are favourable to an individual manager. Unfortunately this is more common than you might believe. A good many people have enjoyed successful careers by being skilled at playing the political game, not by being particularly competent within their own work areas. This generates frustration, particularly among people who take pride in their work and gain satisfaction by creating benefit for the company. They feel a sense of powerlessness and anger when they see people who manipulate managers and budgets gain more responsibility and a growing power base. They are unhappy when they see political gamesmanship grow more important than the company itself, when it becomes more meaningful to gain control of the biggest budgets and districts, to have the nicest offices, the best parking spots, than to achieve the best results.

At one time, I worked for a company that had previously been a state-run monopoly, saddled by a great deal of internal politics. It got me thinking that, in a monopoly where there is no external competition but a large number of skilled and ambitious employees, it may well be that staff members don't know where to direct their energy and creativity. With whom should they compete? In this case, it ended up that members of staff competed with one another, internally, turning their energy and creativity inwards, because no matter what happened, they always had customers. We were the only ones in the market. As a result, politics steered the organization. But only a monopoly can survive this type of situation. Ten to 15 years after government monopolies had been abolished, and the company faced stiff competition, that same internal political focus remained, and as a result, a large number of customers opted to switch to other suppliers.

General Motors, for many years the world's largest company – and still one of the largest – was forced towards bankruptcy in

2009, partly due to an executive culture that prioritized personal power and internal politics over creating value for customers. Had the US government not stepped in with a $50bn bailout, it would definitely have gone bankrupt. And yet, in the end, the executives continued to battle for internal power and awarded one another enormous benefits, even though the company suffered years of losses and falling sales.

I am convinced that, in the long run, there are two factors that outweigh all organizational politics: results and integrity.

Organizations that do not achieve good results are doomed. To survive, you have to deliver something of value to customers and other interested parties, regardless of what you are producing, or the direction of the company. Whether a company is dealing with shareholders, taxpayers, patients, or students, organizations that do not deliver will die, or be replaced by more efficient solutions.

Successful organizations need people who can focus on delivering actual value and who are aware that this requires hard work and even sacrifice at times. These 'bottom line' individuals will, with time, be encouraged and rewarded for what they have achieved in terms of profits. Without them, the processes that create value outside the company will come to a halt.

Integrity and profits go hand in hand. In reality, this is a matter of who you are and who you want to be. Your personal integrity impacts the way others see you, because no one person is greater than the sum of his thoughts, words, and deeds. When I work with executives and leaders in various organizations and use the word integrity – by which I mean the ultimate integrity to yourself – I usually ask them what legacy they want to leave.

Many managers have been highly successful as executives, which to everyone else is impressive, but the question is whether they are equally impressed by their own outcomes. They know the sacrifices they have made and whether their successes have been because they have actually achieved results, or because they have weaseled their way up, using politics. People who involve themselves in political games often appear satisfied enough on the outside, but I often wonder if they feel good about themselves knowing they have stolen credit from others and not created anything of true value within their own professional lives. On the other hand, people who have truly created value are not always the most popular in a company, especially in the upper echelons, and sometimes their image suffers because they have been asked to make tough decisions, based on what has been the best for the company and society in general. In retrospect though, they can regard themselves with pride and with their integrity intact.

Is there any way to reduce, or better still eliminate, negative political behavior? One way is to ignore it, but that gives rise to other problems. Another way is to expose the political games going on in the company. Take the opportunity to engage in an open discussion about internal politics and the advantages or disadvantages of the way politics functions in the company and how this could be improved. Remember to reveal the driving forces behind decisions and the reactions of individuals whenever possible. Even doing this has its risks though. In a highly politicized organization, it is easy to find yourself on the outside, making it difficult to build a successful career if you don't play the game.

But it's better to be outside than to be on the inside, as part of the game, unable to keep your personal integrity and wellbeing intact.

If more people lay bare the political games that are played in organizations and actively focus on creating value for the company, political gamesmanship will be exposed, leading people to question it and ultimately stop it. But this takes time.

Tips to help you achieve real results

1. Focus on creating value for the entire company and for employees, customers, suppliers, and society in general.
2. Define clear-cut objectives. Communicate these often and report results openly.
3. Be flexible. Strategies and goals are not sacred, but the purpose is.
4. Be straightforward and clear in your communications (not pig-headed but clear).
5. Avoid manipulation and 'out' manipulators.

COMMANDMENT 6

Be inspired and inspire others: if you're not passionate about what you do, do something you're passionate about.

Far too many managers and leaders struggle with the question: "Why am I so bad at motivating my employees?" The answer may perhaps not be what you would expect.

The most crucial factor in the motivation process within an organization is that you, as leader, have a passion for your work and a burning desire for what you do. Naturally, the ideal situation in a company is for everyone, managers and non-managers to be motivated.

No matter what abilities or talents an employee has, if they lack motivation, they can never perform to their fullest potential or deliver what is needed to succeed. For that reason, unmotivated employees are bad employees. The same applies to managers and leaders. If you, as a manager, are not passionate about what you do, it impacts on the entire organization. The choices you make affect not only you, but employees, customers, suppliers and many others. If you, as a leader, are not motivated, who is? You cannot inspire your staff if you are not committed to what you are doing. Understanding how those inner driving forces work is extremely important for creative leadership.

If you are not highly committed, your job will feel like any old job. You will not get the personal or job satisfaction that you deserve or the urge to do your very best. I would go as far as to say you won't get the satisfaction *from life* that you deserve, since we spend so much of our lives at work.

If you get stuck in a job you are not passionate about, the biggest loser is you.

To identify the type of manager a person is, determine how much focus he or she places on *results* and *employees*, and whether he or she maintains a good balance between the two. A manager with an extreme focus on results strives to excel and pays little attention to the needs or problems of individuals; many people find this type of manager difficult. It might sound much nicer to have a manager who is highly in tune with the needs of his or her staff and less focused on the bottom line. But in the long run, neither of these types of leader are stimulating for employees because what keeps a company together is a commitment to achieving a common objective. When there is no common objective, and no focus on achieving results, staff are less motivated and do not feel any satisfaction in their jobs. Both of these extreme cases are problematic for people working in the company.

Then there is another type of manager, maybe the worst type: the manager who doesn't care at all, who doesn't really 'see' his or her employees and is not interested in performance. Sometimes, this type of manager is known as the 'apathetic' manager. These leaders make no real demands on the organization and try to weasel as much as possible out of it.

I had a manager like this when I worked at Whirlpool's European office in Italy. He was extremely uncommitted and apathetic and had a few comical ways of managing to do as little as possible. At our office in Italy, employees didn't start work as early in the morning as those of us based in northern Europe, but they worked later into the evening. Although my manager was based in southern Europe and had the later working hours, he would sneak away from the office by 4pm or 5pm most days, but always left a light on in his office. He also hung a sports jacket over the back of his chair, left a little paper strewn around the desk and kept his computer on, so that anyone walking by would think he was working, but had just stepped out of the room. My office faced his, but even so, it took me quite a long time to realize that this was his method of making other people think he was working late.

He was also a master of taking long vacations. In Italy, companies usually have their holiday period in August, and most people were off work at that time – except for my boss. He was pretty clever; he told everyone in the office that he would wait until September to take his holiday. The advantage of his 'sacrifice' would be that he would stay in the office and make sure everything was running when everyone else was away, and in that way, he had almost two months vacation. He hardly every showed up at the office in August. Instead, he demanded that either I, or one of his other subordinates, work in August to keep an eye on things and then he would show up once in a while to check how things were going and to see if anything needed to be handled. In the meantime, he was at home and on holiday.

His lack of commitment was contagious and the entire department was paralyzed and seemingly totally uninterested. "Why care when the boss doesn't care?" was the general attitude. Aside from the ethical issue that he was deceiving his employer, the biggest problem was that he was deceiving his employees. They had a right to expect him to run the operation according to the set objectives. When he didn't do it, his employees also became lethargic and unmotivated.

Edward Deci, a US professor in psychology, and Richard Flaste, a scientific journalist and Pulitzer prize winner, have written a book entitled: *Why We Do What We Do: Understanding Self-Motivation*, looking into the subject of motivation. They were surprised to discover that despite researchers having learned so much about motivation and how motivation works, very little of this information has reached the general public. It turns out that most managers walk around asking themselves how to motivate their employees.

According to Deci and Flaste, studies have identified two types of motivation – intrinsic and extrinsic – and each affects us differently.

Intrinsic motivation is a drive to do something, or to achieve something, and we all have that drive inside us. Intrinsic motivation entails doing something to satisfy that inner urge. To quote Deci and Flaste: "Smelling the roses, being enthralled by how the pieces of a puzzle fit together, seeing the sunlight as it dances in the clouds, feeling the thrill of reaching a mountain summit: these are experiences that need yield nothing more to be fully justified."

Intrinsic motivation occurs whenever the activity or behavior is a reward in itself, and although there may be other rewards involved, it is not these that generate the motivation. A job can offer the opportunity to be rich and famous but if the job itself is so interesting that you would do it even if it did not make you rich or famous, that is intrinsic motivation (see also self-determination theory (SDT); Deci and Ryan, 1985). Motivation at work is embedded in the individual and relates to how you enjoy your job and your work duties, and it has a proven effect on job productivity.

Extrinsic motivation involves the drive to do something that offers some type of external reward, such as a bonus or commission, outside of the individual. This is where we have to differentiate between motivation and motivational factors. In this example, money is a motivational factor that can create motivation in an individual, but motivation stems from each person's attitude towards the motivational factor. Suppose someone who was not particularly interested in money was working as a salesman in a company with a comprehensive commission programme. If the salesman really liked meeting customers and helping them solve their problems, but was not significantly influenced by a commission-based programme, they would still be a good salesman. A salesman who was motivated by this type of reward system would place heavy emphasis on getting the order.

Suppose the salesman didn't care that much about commission, nor enjoy sales. Neither the commission nor the sales process would make much of a difference to him. In the case of this salesman, he may not enjoy his work, it may just be a way to earn money. In his case, there is a high risk that he might be tempted to focus on selling as much as possible in the short term, rather than building up long-term positive relationships with customers.

In the case of sales commissions, I have often wondered whether the commissions programmes exist to motivate salespeople or to protect employers from having to pay excessive salaries to people who do not sell well. The most valuable salespeople sell well regardless of whether they make commission or not. I don't think I have ever met an employer who had anything against paying a good salary to a top-performing salesman but they do not want to pay an under-performing employee a high salary.

Regardless of this, at best, your intrinsic motivation is not influenced by external motivational factors such as a new bonus or commission system or a sales kickoff to entice everyone to work harder. Yes, that's right, I said your intrinsic motivation, at best, is *not* influenced by external factors, and at worst, these external factors can be inhibiting. What managers don't know is that external motivation factors risk having a greater negative impact on motivation than a positive one.

It is likely that extrinsic motivational factors will create barriers that keep employees from being motivated rather than boosting their motivation. Initiatives designed to improve motivation can have the opposite effect.

But why is that so? I have pondered why I felt less motivated after motivational kickoff meetings than before I went to them. This has happened even when a great deal of effort has been invested in inducing motivation. It made no difference what kind of activities were offered or how they phrased the words. I felt it was intrusive, as if someone was trying to force me to be motivated. A fairly normal response from people in that kind of a situation is to be on guard. When external forces attempt to influence our motivation, it is normal to rebel against these forces. In this way, we understand that extrinsic motivation has very little effect on us, or has a negative effect.

External factors attempt to create *compliance*. Because, if we're perfectly honest here, isn't that the purpose behind all managers' well-intended attempts to motivate us – to engender compliance? To ensure we comply with company objectives, stand straight in line and do what they want us to do? Researchers claim that when you use compliance as a motivational tool, defiance will almost always be the response.

A compliance/defiance reaction is perhaps not too difficult to understand. When someone else tries to control us, to get us to do what they want us to do, instead of what we want to do, there is a pretty good chance we will react defiantly. The secret lies in helping employees to understand why they should want the same thing as the company. What you need to do, quite simply, is to align the interests of the company with those of its employees. If staff interests are not aligned to those of the organization, motivation, and thereby productivity, will falter. In an ideal world, in which individuals only work on those things in which they are truly interested and everyone has the same objectives, motivation will take care of itself. But the reality is not perfect, and not all managers have chosen their professions or workplaces based on their passions.

I usually advise managers to halt all attempts at motivating employees, and instead, to try to inspire them. I suggest they let their team members be responsible for their own motivation, just as they should take care of their own motivation. Make sure you are in the right profession and the right place to gain an outlet for your motivation. Once you have figured that out, you can help others find their motivation, either at work or somewhere else.

As a leader, you can offer people opportunities to satisfy their inner drive and will by inspiring them. You can plant seeds and trigger ideas and questions, but it is up to individual staff members to decide for themselves what they will do with these. The difference between motivation and inspiration may appear marginal, but it is, in fact, considerable. Individuals are responsible for their own motivation, while inspiration can spring from a variety of different sources, including managers.

We can all be inspired by things that, ultimately, we are not motivated to do anything about. Ten years after graduating from high school, I attended a class reunion. I had already moved to Sweden by this time, and was working for a global corporation. I travelled for work quite a lot and enjoyed a pretty exciting work life. When I sat down and reminisced with an old classmate, he said he wished he could do what I had done: move to a different country and culture and experience something new and exciting. I replied that there are plenty of flights that leave every day from our old hometown to all conceivable corners of the world.

Years later, I met him again when I returned to the US for a visit, and he said more or less the same thing. My experiences were clearly something that inspired him, but something in which he wasn't really prepared to invest.

I usually say that the difference between inspiration and motivation is perspiration. If you are genuinely motivated, you will do something about it. When I was young, I used to joke about becoming a rock star. My mother was a music teacher and I grew up in a home filled with music. I did a lot of singing but I was never serious about a singing career. Being a rock star was just a fantasy that I have never felt a true desire to realize. It is fun to entertain fantasies, we all need them, but it is not until you are ready to act that your fantasy moves from inspiration to motivation and is transformed into a vision, with goals that you strive to achieve. My rock star fantasy will remain a fantasy – apart from when someone hands me a microphone at a party and I torture everyone around me for a while.

Deci and Flaste put it this way:

As managers, instead of asking how we can motivate people, we should be asking: "How can we create the conditions within which people will motivate themselves?"

I was mentor to the president of a medium-sized company and he was worried that his employees were not motivated. He discussed various classical steps to boost motivation, such as making kick-off events more fun, bringing in coffee and doughnuts, or putting up posters filled with inspirational slogans; maybe even moving towards individual bonus objectives. I told him I understood what he meant but thought he was wrong about the motivation part. His members of staff were already highly motivated, but not necessarily about their work. They were strongly involved in their non-work-related activities, children, vacation plans, summer cottages, churches, boats and so on. These motivated them to put up with their boring jobs at the company so they could finance all the things that did motivate them. And that is what is called being motivated. The problem was that the employees could find no outlet for their motivation at work. Many studies point to the fact that employees who are motivated at work are not only more productive, but substantially more productive. For that reason, the president who wanted his employees to feel a greater sense of engagement was right, but the answer was not to attempt to increase their motivation, but to ask himself why his people did not have an outlet for their motivation at work and what he could do about that.

Edward Deci and Richard Flaste have produced a model in the shape of a triangle, that shows the three fundamental concepts for motivation.

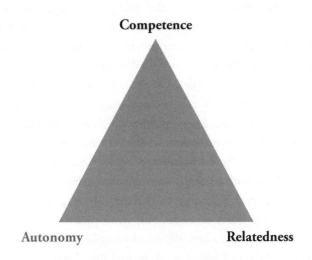

Competence

Autonomy   **Relatedness**

Key Elements of Intrinsic Motivation
Deci, E L and Ryan, R M (1985). Intrinsic motivation and self-determination in human behavior. New York: Plenum

Competence, autonomy (self-determination) and relatedness (sense of belonging) are the cornerstones of motivation. If I, as a manager, wanted to help a colleague find an outlet for his or her work motivation, I would look into how I could help people to improve their skills or competence. Employees who feel they are not very good at their jobs do not feel any strong motivation, while those who have mastered their jobs find it satisfying and are motivated to do more.

A manager can boost an employee's competence in various ways, including introducing education, on-the-job training and other opportunities for development. As the skills of an employee increase in relation to their work duties, so will their motivation. Bear in mind that the manager, in this instance, does not create motivation in his or her employees. The manager simply ensures that staff have the right conditions under which to find an outlet for motivation within their work.

The other two corners of the triangle are more convoluted, which is the result of our own complexity. On the one hand, we want a high degree of self-determination – none of us thinks it is particularly inspiring to be controlled or to have others interfering in how we perform our roles. On the other hand, we want to feel part of the group. I have met many managers who have expressed their frustration at not knowing how much freedom they should give their staff, to increase their level of self-determination, and to what extent they should monitor people, to ensure they comply with company work methods and rules. In today's companies, we invest a great deal of energy in charting, developing and implementing standardized processes and work procedures. The question is: can you create a high degree of autonomy without crippling the company's standardized work procedures? I would argue that you definitely can!

I talked about this issue at a conference and a woman approached me afterwards, telling me she was a sales manager for a large insurance company. She explained that she wanted to give her sales staff greater influence, but felt it wouldn't work in her company.

"I am given a budget from my managers and I have to divide it among the sales people," she said. "I have very little say in the matter and just receive a sales target and that is the figure I have to use. So what can I do to give my sales people more autonomy?"

At that time, I was in charge of sales for Volvo Cars and I told her we were in a similar position. I also was given a budget and was told how many cars we had to sell and how much money we should make. But instead of dividing up the budget among my subordinate regional managers and giving them a directive, regarding set targets, I told them about the goals of the budget I had received and asked them: "Can you divide up the budget between yourselves and come up with a plan on how we can deliver it?" I left them to work it out in peace and the regional managers later presented their joint proposal, which was not far off of the one I would have drawn up. The difference was that I did not come up with the proposal, they did. Naturally, their motivation to achieve the goals was much greater because they had been involved in setting them.

Even though my superiors had acted in a way I thought was wrong, this did not mean I had to act in a similar way towards the people I managed. Neither did it mean I had no say in the work of the regional managers. Obviously, as their manager, I had a part in the discussion, but the fact of the matter was that I very seldom had to step in and make adjustments to the decisions made or activities carried out by my subordinates.

What is interesting about self-determination is that it engenders a greater sense of belonging. When staff members are given more autonomy, can set their own goals and decide how to achieve them, they feel more a part of the process. Nothing makes a person feel more excluded than the knowledge that they have very little to say in matters, and a boss whose approach is "here are your goals and you had better reach them!" In this scenario, there is no room for comment, adjustment, departure, alternatives or suggestions from employees. They are expected to work, not to think. As a result, staff feel their organization has little confidence in them.

In the case of Volvo, where I had given the regional managers greater opportunity to change their goals, they felt much more a part of the organization, which was also demonstrated by the sales results.

Having studied Deci and Flaste's triangle and gained insight into motivation for individuals, we can examine a triangle by a Swedish researcher named Sven Kylén. In his book *Working groups with development and change* assignment, he suggests that what characterizes smooth-running groups is the balance between the group's need to achieve certain results and individual group members' needs for autonomy and belonging. The results the group strives to achieve are determined by the goals agreed by the individuals, which in turn contribute to fulfilling the organization's purpose.

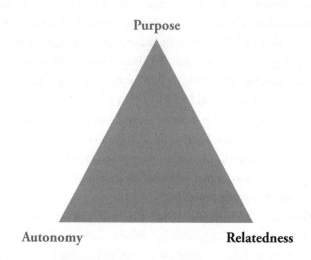

Purpose

Autonomy   **Relatedness**

Organizational Performance Model
Sven Kylén (1993) Work Groups with development and change assignments: from defensive to offensive routines. Institute of Psychology, The University of Gothenberg.

For a group to function effectively, Kylén maintains that an individual must feel a high degree of autonomy, a mandate to do their job, but also a strong sense of collaboration with other members of the group. This 'we' feeling shouldn't be confused with everyone liking one another, a cosy atmosphere surrounding the business. This is about group members having a sense of a definite, strong bond, which binds them together in their efforts to achieve the goals and objectives of the company.

All three of these components affect one other. The 'common' purpose enhances our sense of inclusion. There may be nothing that molds a group together like the feeling of having something important to fight for together (for example, winning a medal, curing a disease, meeting the company's goals for the year). As I described earlier, this increased autonomy contributes to a sense of belonging, just like when an individual sets his or her own goals.

But autonomy is also a precondition for achieving results. To succeed in reaching challenging goals, each member of staff must have the power and opportunity to contribute to doing so. And when goals are reached, the group 'we' feeling is enhanced even further. There is a terrific feeling that arises from achieving something challenging together. Battling side-by-side, and achieving results, can build an incredibly strong bond. I have experienced this many times in my professional life, but a particular instance that strongly affected me was when I was at Whirlpool, working for several years with a group

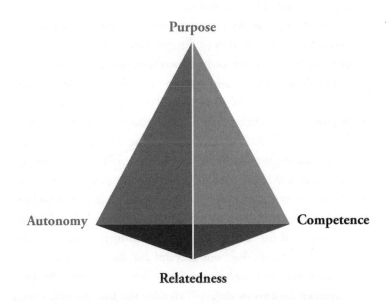

The Individual/Organizational Performance Model
Individuals invest and unite their intrinsic motivation
around a common purpose. Kelly Odell

of people whose aim was to save the unprofitable, closure-threatened, microwave division. I will never forget the feeling I experienced when group management decided not to close down the operation. The project created an enormous sense of 'we' between all of us working on it, and many of us still feel a strong bond, 20 years later.

After taking a closer look at the two triangles, it struck me that two of the corners in Deci and Flastes' triangle (figure 2, page 99) were the same as the corners in Kylén's triangle (figure 3, page 102): autonomy and relatedness. This led me to wonder whether you could merge the two triangles to demonstrate the connection between the individual and the group in a tetrahedron (figure 4, page 103). The base of the tetrahedron – the motivational triangle formed by Deci and Flaste, comprising autonomy, relatedness and competence – demonstrates the individual perspective that says that even if we, as individuals, are motivated by different things, we are all motivated by something.

Kylén's triangle shows a group perspective, and by merging the two triangles, the description of the motivated individuals is transformed into a description of high-performing groups. The top of the tetrahedron, which is also the top of Kylén's triangle, is where you find the term 'results' (which can be used to mean objectives or purpose in this context). This shows that it is only when we, as motivated individuals, can agree on working together to achieve a common goal or purpose that we can become a functioning group.

The Deci and Flaste triangle is intended to describe the needs that drive intrinsic motivation in individuals, so does not include the group perspective. Kylén's triangle is only intended to describe the group's need for balance between autonomy, relatedness and results, and therefore does not account for the individual's need for competence, in order to maximize his motivation. By putting together the two models, we identify the four factors, which include both the individual and group perspectives in a successful organization. If we want to succeed in our business, we need to support our employees' motivation by boosting their autonomy, relatedness and competence within the framework of clear, understandable and agreed-upon goals, objectives and/or purposes.

One definition I like to use is that "an organization is a context where people cooperate of their own free will to achieve common objectives". Two vital criteria for an organization of any kind are objectives, and individuals who are prepared to try to achieve those objectives. If the individuals are not prepared to achieve those objectives, then by definition, you do not have a functioning organization. But if the individuals do not agree on common goals or purposes, this does not mean they are not motivated, only that they are not motivated to achieve the same things.

An organization may have many employees. But the fact that people share offices and earn salaries from the same company does not automatically signify a coherent organization. More is needed. I usually go so far as to maintain that organizations are only imaginary. It makes no difference whether it involves a company, a university or a kennel club. Organizations are only theoretical constructions that we make up in order to make life easier. If you register a company, you have created a legal entity, not a real entity.

The only thing that is real in the company is you and me. People who choose to cooperate to achieve common goals or purposes are the only reality in any organization.

When a group of people discovers a common passion for keeping bees and members feel like spending their leisure time together promoting knowledge about bees and beekeeping, they have created an enterprise. The fact that they may, at some point, decide to register their club as a legal entity, in order to deal with expenditure and revenue, is only a practical step to facilitate the activity.

Organizations are fabrications, while people are real. Even if you don't fully buy into this theory, we can hopefully agree that an organization in which participants cannot agree on common goals, and do not want to work together, is, at best, dysfunctional.

When I was the head of Whirlpool in Sweden, we had two policies, which were somewhat contradictory. On the one hand, the salespeople's bonuses were based on the proportion of gross profits they generated through their sales efforts, rather than on overall sales volumes – which may not be particularly unusual. But on the other hand, we were not allowed to disclose the manufacturing costs for the products. This meant the salespeople did not know what the gross profit was or how much they made on various products. The explanation I was given was that a sales person could quit and start working for a competitor and take the information on manufacturing costs with them, which could hurt us. I found this reasoning a bit odd since our main competitors pretty much already knew what our costs were for the different products. We were competing in a mature industry, where the products were fairly similar to one another, and our competitors manufactured their products in similar ways to us, and mostly in the same countries.

A number of attempts were made to steer the sales staff to more profitable sales by listing certain products as gold, silver or bronze products. Each of these methods proved complicated and ineffective. The salespeople couldn't understand why they were being steered and rewarded based on profitability, but were not privy to the information they needed to succeed. In the end, I (and a few of the other country managers) decided to buck the system and give our sales staff access to the calculations they needed.

In the space of just a few months, there was a clear improvement in profitability in those countries that had given the sales people access to this information. The sales teams also appeared happier and more motivated.

A few months later, the rule was changed so that all country managers could share product costs with their salespeople. One salesman told me that he had always felt that the company had lacked faith in him, or regarded him as a less important member of the company. Now he felt a part of the organization and was more successful too.

In other words, by changing the rules slightly, regarding the handling of specific information, we established conditions under which staff were able to find an outlet for their motivation. They felt a heightened sense of competence, relatedness and autonomy.

Ultimately, you alone are responsible for your own motivation at work. If you end up in a job you do not enjoy, figure out what you want to do instead and what it takes to get there. If you like your job, but are working in an organization that does not function properly, or in which you have no outlet for your own motivation (due to the boss, the culture, or the rules), either work to improve the situation or find another job. I usually fall back on this simple rule to remind myself that I actually am in control of my own fate. In all situations, you only have three choices:

accept the environment – change the environment – change environments.

Imagine being in a job that is imperfect, but where you decide to accept the situation. This is not the same as saying you are apathetic or don't care about the organization. Accepting the situation means you accept things as they are and actively work to realize the goals of the organization. If there are factors that you neither can, nor want, to accept, you can decide to improve the situation proactively, for example, by trying to change rules and improve processes.

You should always have the opportunity to say what you think, and often there are more opportunities than you realize. Sharing your ideas and views about the current situation with your managers and colleagues can help improve things. If you recognize a problem in your organization, it is likely that others share your view. Even individuals at lower levels within the organizational hierarchy can act as catalysts for changes that have positive long-term effects on the entire organization. If, in the end, you cannot or do not want to engineer the changes needed so that you can enjoy your work, perhaps you should change environments completely; in other words, change jobs.

After one of my lectures, a woman asked me whether I could give her some advice on how to deal with a particular situation at her place of work. Then she spent ten minutes explaining how awful her manager was. I have to admit, I was shocked. Her tale seemed to epitomize every possible fault a manager can have. I realized that I only heard one side of the story (and there are always two sides), but even if only half of what she said was true, she had, without a doubt, one of the worst managers I have ever heard about.

Her question to me was straight and simple:

"What do you think I should do?"

Sometimes I feel like the Oracle of Delphi, but sometimes I wish I had better advice to give. The only thing I could come up with this time was:

"Accept the environment, change the environment, or change environments."

She looked at me a little puzzled. I explained that it sounded as if the situation was too difficult for her to accept as it was, and she agreed. So I asked whether she had done anything to improve the situation, such as talking to her manager and telling him how she felt about him and his leadership (or lack thereof).

She looked at me in shock and said her manager was crazy and impossible to talk to. Then I asked her if she had spoken with her boss's boss or with someone in her union, or in the HR department. It turned out she had not spoken to anyone about it. When asked why, she said she was afraid to stir the pot, in case it caused her to get fired. I explained to her that it seemed that the only option she had left was to find another job. If she was not prepared to improve her job situation and did not want to switch jobs, she ultimately had to accept the situation and that she would be working under the 'boss from hell'. She was not responsible for her manager's terrible behavior, but she was responsible for continuing in that situation.

When speaking at another management conference, a woman told me she was not happy in her job, but added that there were not that many jobs to choose from in her small town. I asked whether she was forced to stay in that town. It was a nice place, but most of the world's population didn't live there, and they were no less happy for that. She said that her husband was a senior executive at a major corporation in her town. I asked her whether she was forced to live and work in the same town as her husband. I know many couples where one works in one city, the other in another, and at weekends they meet at a hotel somewhere in between. She explained that her grown-up children lived in that small town as well, and that she was active in various clubs there and had many friends and a large social life locally.

The way I saw it was that she had taken stock of her life. On the minus side, she had a job she didn't like, but on the plus side, she had plenty of advantages. When she weighed the pluses against the minuses, she felt it was a reasonable sacrifice to accept the situation at work in order to enjoy the positives of living in her home town. The only thing she had not done was accept and take responsibility for the decision she had made to persevere at a less-than-enjoyable job so as to enjoy everything else in life.

Once she accepted responsibility for that decision, something remarkable would happen. She would probably begin to enjoy her job more. As long as she felt she was trapped in a boring job, there was a greater chance that her frustration would grow. When she felt like a victim, unable to change anything, she might well become resigned and depressed. When she acknowledged that she had chosen to place herself in this situation, and that she wasn't a victim, she realized her job was an important piece of her 'life puzzle', even if it wasn't the most enjoyable piece.

Another factor that been proven to influence our level of motivation at work and our productivity is meaning.

In recent years, leadership, and motivational literature has seen more and more discussion of the term 'happiness'. The belief is that, if you are happy at work, you are more motivated and therefore more productive. Although this may well be true, research indicates that 'happiness' is only the product of, or symptom of, something else: meaning. It turns out that people who believe they, or their organization, are doing something important are happier and more motivated at work.

Gallup, the global research and analytics company, has identified 12 factors that appear to be integral to the success of organizations. By conducting more than 10 million interviews with employees over the course of many years, Gallup discovered a correlation between how employees feel about these 12 factors and the success of the company (Wagner and Harter, 2006). One of these factors is believing what your company does is important. It seems that we should focus more attention on giving jobs meaning rather than on trying to create happiness.

Imagine working for a company that discovered a cure for cancer or AIDS. Most of us would, no doubt, feel this work to be important and we might be more inclined to put up with unattractive office space or lower salaries in order to participate in it. There is risk, however, that after a while, we might forget the purpose of our work and begin regarding it as just a job.

On one occasion, I was speaking to a company that made dialysis machines. When preparing my talk, I spoke with the head of the unit at the company and asked him if there was anything he thought I should bear in mind. He responded that his employees often forgot they were involved in something important. For me, as an outsider, that seemed highly unlikely.

"Dialysis machines are not only important, they are critical to the survival of the people who depend on them," I said. "How could anyone not remember that?"

He explained: "Imagine a situation in which one of our technicians visits a hospital or a clinic to service or repair a machine. The technician enters a room where the machine is located, replaces the necessary spare parts and then leaves. Only after the technician has left does a patient enter the room and get hooked up to the machine. Thanks to the dialysis machine, the patient is able to live, have a meaningful job – to be a mother to her children."

When he explained this to me, I was touched and asked whether he had brought up stories like this with his technicians. He admitted that he hadn't, and I suggested he should start doing so. His most important job was to help his employees to stay focused on the purpose of the company, and how vital it was to society.

At this point I should emphasize that the inherent meaning in, or importance of, our work is based on our individual perceptions. It is the individual's own view of a situation that counts, not the perceptions of the rest of the world.

This became abundantly clear to me when I was speaking at a conference and said something along the lines of: "All organizations in society are important.... as long as you're working with cigarettes". A man in the audience got to his feet and responded that cigarettes were definitely important. He explained that he worked for a well-known tobacco company and that, in a world in which society tries to make us conform to its ideal, cigarettes are one of the last means of expression of individualism.

I felt he truly believed in his work. He was thoroughly convinced that what he did was vital, and he was both happy and motivated. What I thought, or what other people might have thought, was of no consequence; the most important thing was his perception, based on his unique world view and values.

Another time, I was asked to speak at a management conference for a company that made military weapons. When I met the men who had contracted me to discuss the talk, they explained they were in the midst of a project designed to change the culture of the company. One of the things they wanted to do was to generate a sense that the work they were doing was important to society. They thought that would boost people's job satisfaction and motivation. They wanted me to explain how leaders could create a stronger association between the company's vision and values, its purpose in society and the employees' view of their jobs.

One of the questions I asked them was how they justified the fact that the products they developed and manufactured were designed to kill people. I had read parts of a document in which they wrote about a weapon's 'payload', a term used to express how efficient (deadly) a weapon is. I told them that, to be able to work there, you had to hold the view that these weapons were a vital and necessary evil. Perhaps you had to believe you were creating conditions for world peace by giving people the chance to defend themselves, and to create a power balance in the world. The looks I got from these people were enough to tell me that I was not going to get the assignment. They made it very clear to me that they did not intend to touch upon issues like that. I feel that if a leader is not honest enough to admit to the purpose of an operation, and stand by it, the chances of making the employees proud of it are small indeed.

If you do not feel your company fulfills a vital function in society, you should talk to one another and develop an understanding of your purpose. If you still do not feel it is important to you, then you should find something else to do.

Tips to help you to inspire others

1. Be honest with yourself about what you want and why you are working where you are.
2. Encourage yourself, and others, to either create the job you want, or go and get it.
3. Stop trying to motivate others. Inspire and help them to gain an outlet for their own motivation.
4. Invest time and money in the competence of your people, increase their self-determination, and involve them deeper in the company's life.

COMMANDMENT 7

Base decisions on facts: intuition is better than no information, but facts are best.

THis does not feel right. I don't believe in this," said the top executive, and the decision was made.

You might be surprised to discover that many crucial decisions in our organizations are based on 'intuition, rather than facts. I worked in a company in which the CEO spoke out in a number of magazine and newspaper interviews:

"I run the company on intuition!"

And he did.

I was vice president of marketing for this company, and the CEO gave two of my highly capable employees the task of developing an advanced market analysis, which they worked on for six months. They did a fantastic job. When they presented to the CEO, providing a summary of their conclusions, he said:

"This does not feel right. I don't believe in this."

He then said something about the report not matching his gut feeling. Everyone in the room was stunned. Two highly talented strategists had invested time and energy in this analysis and he had dismissed it with his gut feeling. I grew irritated and couldn't keep quiet.

"With all due respect to your gut feeling, it is not sufficient simply to dismiss this work," I said. "Considering your knowledge of the business and your long experience, your gut feeling may well be a signal that there is something we should take a closer look at or question, but you have to be more specific about what you are trying to say."

He was prepared to ignore the entire analysis. In the end, with some effort, we were able to discuss the analysis and arrive more precisely at what it was that did not feel right to him. Ultimately, we were able to continue along the lines my staff's analysis indicated.

For a number of years, there has been a trend promoting the idea of letting common sense dictate decisions. But imagine the chaos there would be if everyone relied on their own common sense and gut feelings.

Our intuition is related to our own experience, which means that various individuals, with their own unique experiences, will arrive at different conclusions, based on their own intuition. How do we know how much common sense we really have in common? If different people's common sense tells them different things, whose common sense should we trust? What are our assumptions based on?

That is not to say I think that intuition is a bad thing, but it can never replace facts and information. Executives who rely solely, or primarily, on their gut feelings are often covering up their own laziness. They have not bothered, or had the urge, to study the information available, and so they walk into meetings unprepared with the attitude that their gut feeling is the most important decision-making factor.

How many meetings have you attended where whoever is making a presentation more or less reads the material verbatim for the group, despite the fact that everyone in the room has had access to it for a couple of weeks prior to the meeting? Instead of discussing the decision based on the information available, the information itself is discussed and then a decision is made in haste, in order to make it in time for the next meeting. I maintain that this is often the result of not doing your homework.

Leaders and managers who base their decisions on intuition and gut feeling are far more common than you would imagine. So how can companies be so successful when many decisions are based on that 'special little feeling' executives have in their stomachs? The answer is that, in an industry where many important decisions are made more or less by guessing, the best guesser wins.

There is reason to believe that our intuition is, at least partly, genetically programmed to produce different responses to the same question. Some researchers argue that, in certain situations, this phenomenon may be helpful for the survival of our species. When cavemen were attacked by a wild animal, some instinctively stood still, others played dead, a few ran, and some attacked the animal. This strategy increased the likelihood that some people would survive, although others were sacrificed. Even today, we see that when there is an earthquake, some people hide under their beds or desks, while others run out into the street. Here again, people's reactions increase the chances that not everyone will die in the same catastrophe. This may well be the rationale for the human species as a whole, but it is hardly a logical strategy for the individual.

Today, we know there are both good and bad strategies taken by people confronted with wild animals or earthquakes. Some increase the chances of survival, others reduce them. People living in earthquake-prone regions learn the best way to react to survive; in a similar way, having grown up in Oklahoma, I learned the best way to survive tornadoes. By the same token, decision makers should teach themselves how to make better and better decisions. Study facts, learn from history and develop better plans of action. Acting primarily on intuition might be slightly better than tossing a coin, but not much.

I don't know how many times I have heard people argue totally different points of view, each claiming that their perspective is based on common sense. Without facts and thorough analysis, this is like a guessing game where whoever guesses a little better, or makes the best argument, wins. Or the person in the room with the most power makes the decision based on his or her common sense, and then hopes that everything will be fine.

One example of a poor intuitive decision was when the 7-Eleven convenience stores discovered customer satisfaction had declined. The chain came to the conclusion that it had to boost the enthusiasm of in-store employees. 7-Eleven invested enormous quantities of money in sending staff on courses, teaching them better customer service and 'charm'. The courses delivered what they promised and staff became much more customer friendly. But customer satisfaction continued to slide and no one could explain why.

After further analysis, it was discovered that being served by charming staff wasn't a priority for 7-Eleven customers. They wanted fast, easy service; to fill their car with gas, dash into the store, fill their flask with coffee or buy something cold to drink, pay, and leave quickly. But when staff members were nicer and more talkative, it took longer at the cash register and queues grew, and that was something customers did not like. Naturally, customers were not opposed to a pleasant greeting from staff members, and maybe a smile, but not at the expense of speed.

Just like the 7-Eleven executives, most people might consider it a good idea to send store staff to customer service courses. But through conducting well-researched analysis, based on facts, you would arrive at an entirely different conclusion; for example, they could have gained a better understanding of customers' real needs and put in place processes to speed customer service. What everyone assumed to be the right solution to the problem became an obstacle, preventing the chain from boosting customer satisfaction. A careful analysis of the real reasons behind the chain's declining customer satisfaction might well have led to simplified, faster check-out routines or changes in store layout.

Intuition is an extension of our competence and knowledge. Intuition can help us to formulate questions and find answers to a question but decisions should, as far as possible, be based on facts.

In Malcolm Gladwell's book *Blink: The Power of Thinking Without Thinking*, he writes about the ability to make decisions in "the blink of an eye". As an example, he uses the time when the J Paul Getty Museum in California purchased an ancient, and extremely rare, Greek statue – a kouros – for US$10m. Before making the purchase, the museum authenticated the statue and all the documents and paperwork were in order. Everything seemed correct. But the first time this extremely costly statue was put on display for a few prominent experts, they had the feeling something was wrong. They had the feeling immediately and instinctively. New studies were conducted and it turned out that a number of the documents had been falsified and that the statue was probably a fake.

This demonstrates two things. The first thing we should acknowledge in this example is that it was experts who sensed that something was not right, people with a high level of knowledge and experience in that field. Their intuition was an extension of their competence. Had they shown the statue to ordinary people on the street and asked them whether they thought it was genuine or fake, the answers would probably have been highly mixed. Second, a gut feeling would not have been sufficient to claim that the statue was a fake, but it signalled that it was worth re-examining in more detail. This subtle difference is important, because intuition alone did not make it possible to know whether the statue was a fake. The experts had a feeling that something was amiss, which led to a fact-based re-examination of the statue. The results indicated there was something wrong, and facts led to the conclusion that the statue was indeed a forgery.

Psychologist Daniel Kahneman, who won the Nobel Prize in Economics in 2002, gives a subtler picture of the notion of intuition. His ground-breaking work on decision making and risk assessment proves that people are not particularly rational. In Kahneman's book, *Thinking Fast and Slow*, he explains that people's intellects can be divided into two different parts that he calls system 1 and system 2.

System 1 encompasses the part of our intellect that helps us make decisions in a 'blink' as Gladwell would put it, but that part of our intellect is very often wrong. Kahneman writes that system 1 is the part of our intellect that enables an experienced car driver to hold a conversation with a passenger while driving, provided the traffic is not busy and nothing unexpected happens. If the driver suddenly has to step hard on the brakes or pass a trailer truck, it is much more difficult to continue the conversation. That is when system 2 takes over the intellect.

The system 2 intellect is analytical; it seeks alternatives and weighs these against one another. The system 2 intellect requires more focus and more work. When system 2 assumes control, the heartbeat quickens and the pupils dilate. To put it simply, system 1 functions well when we have to make fast decisions about things in which we are knowledgeable and experienced (when we are competent). But system 1 does not work well when we have to make decisions about more complex issues outside of our competence. System 1 can easily come up with the answer to 2 x 2 but system 2 takes over if we need to calculate the answer to 341 x 567. Kahneman argues, scientifically and convincingly, that system 1 intellect, or our intuition, fills a vital function in simplifying our everyday lives, but was never intended to solve complex and challenging problems.

We constantly make mistakes and are easily fooled. In particular, we make mistakes when judging situations in haste, in our intuitive mode. But there is a difference between a mistake and a poor decision. If we have not done our analysis, or the hard work needed to arrive at a good decision, then we do not have good information upon which to base a decision. We should not encourage hasty decisions, where guesswork and assumptions are expected to provide an accurate answer, and then act upon it as if the decision was based on fact.

The chances of making poor decisions rise markedly when analysis is replaced with intuition. Relying on your gut feeling is a bad decision, not a mistake.

During economic downturns, many poor decisions are made. The constant hunt for cost-savings by many companies when sales drop often leads to bad decisions, made intuitively, instead of decisions based on solid information and facts. Many managers intuitively believe that high costs are the problem and that staff and training cutbacks are the answer to declining profits. I have worked in companies that have spent a great deal of money laying off employees only to find themselves, a year or so later, investing large amounts in recruiting and training new staff. And that is an example of a bad decision.

Many companies intuitively reduce training budgets, failing to realize that companies that invest in additional training for their employees are in a much better position coming out of an economic slowdown. That is also a poor decision.

In July 2009, I wrote an opinion piece in Sweden's leading daily newspaper (*Dagens Nyheter*) headlined "Many executives who lead companies do not measure up in a crisis". The article described how people make the wrong choices during economic slumps. As a result of the article, people told me about remarkable and expensive reactions to a downturn in various companies that appeared reasonable on an intuitive level, but upon closer analysis, proved to be wrong.

Intuitive assumptions can be 'truths' of which everyone is aware, without anyone actually knowing the background or if they are based on facts.

Sometimes, it is when we are most confident that we are following a truly fact-based path that we fall into the biggest potholes of intuition. A scientific process or methodology can only be scientific if the entire process is scientifically rigorous. If, at any step in the process, we mix in 'rules of thumb', educated guesses or gut feelings, it can no longer be called scientific.

When considering the people in our organizations, we need to be particularly vigilant and avoid the pitfalls of pseudo-scientific methodology and quasi fact-based analysis. It is not always the experts who discover the most creative solutions. Expertise is usually necessary to solve complicated problems but it can be a big advantage to mix in a few 'wildcards'. Too much knowledge about a specific context can sometimes limit our ability to think 'outside the box'. Non-experts can ask all the stupid questions that jog or inspire the creativity of the experts.

It is almost impossible for an organization to identify the right steps for future development without a real understanding of the past. Qualified guesses and hypotheses are fine for filling in the gaps in a solid analysis, but these educated guesses should be the exception, not the rule, and should be made by competent people, with considerable knowledge and experience in the specific matter.

So, where does intuition really fit into our companies? As I mentioned earlier, intuition is an extension of our knowledge and competence. In other words, our intuition works best in dealing with matters we know something about and is at its worst in areas where we are weak. A doctor's intuition about a patient's health is likely to be far better than a plumber's, but a plumber's intuition about a problem in the sewer system is no doubt better than a doctor's.

There are few situations in which you have access to all the facts. When we analyze a problem and gather the facts, there will always be information missing. Our analyses are never perfect. Sometimes, we may not be able to find the information we need. Perhaps we don't have the time or money to conduct a major study into understanding exactly how our customers feel about a given change in our product offering. Or maybe we have simply missed something. Perhaps we didn't understand a piece of information that would have had a major bearing on the decision. For whatever reason, we almost always have incomplete information and we have to fill in the gaps with assumptions or guesses in order to arrive at a conclusion. That is when you have to ask those people with the most knowledge in the area to use their intuition. This is not instead of facts, but in place of a lack of facts. It is better to have an analysis that is 99% based on facts and where the final 1% is based on the intuition of a competent employee, than to have an analysis based on one 100% wild conjecture.

On one occasion, I was invited to a meeting with the executive management of TeliaSonera. One of the executives presented an investment proposal and our CEO got hung up on a minor calculation error in the analysis. Unfortunately, the executive presenting the material was not familiar enough with the details to be able to handle the president's questions, and the entire meeting was on the verge of derailing. I turned to our president and explained that the miscalculation actually had no major bearing on the conclusions of investment analysis. I told him that no matter how we twisted and turned it, it was still a billion-dollar deal. He wondered how I knew that, and I responded that we had a 50% market share of pretty much everything we sold. In all probability, we would achieve the same with this new service. There are approximately 4 million households in Sweden, so 2 million would be our customers, paying $40 a month for the service. That would give us sales in the region of $1bn. The president asked me how I knew we would be able to charge $40 a month for the subscription. I looked him in the eyes and said:

"I am the vice president of marketing. I am supposed to know things like that."

For a brief moment, the room went silent. The president flipped through his papers before conceding that I was probably right and we could continue our meeting.

In this position, I had been immersed in data from a number of studies and analyses, which carefully examined how much customers were prepared to pay for the service and how many would be interested in buying it. The executive's investment proposal had been thoroughly prepared and a miscalculation of $1m had no bearing on the overall picture. So, an intuitive guess by an expert in the area enabled us to make a decision and move on. In the end, we discovered we were all wrong. The service generated much more than what we expected it would.

All too often, these 'truths' are no more than myths and nonsense. Let's face it, most of us harbour all kinds of theories about organizations and the people in them, and most of those theories are more or less intuitive. In fact, we may be so confident in our 'beliefs' that we never even reflect over whether or not they are actually true. In their book *Hard Facts, Dangerous Half-Truths And Total Nonsense: Profiting From Evidence-Based Management*, Jeffrey Pfefferoch and Robert I Sutton identify the lack of "fact-based management" as one of the greatest risks facing organizations.

Experiment with Boundaries and Limitations: Bigger, Smaller

Expressions such as "you can't see the wood for the trees" and "think outside the box" are particularly applicable to creativity. Our greatest challenge with regard to creativity is not that we lack the ability to come up with creative solutions to problems. Our problem is often that we fail to overcome the fictional mental barriers that limit our creative playing field. Had we truly believed the world was flat, there would have been no reason to think about sailing around it.

Years ago, I spoke at a conference of colleagues from the telecommunications industry. One of the questions I threw out to the audience was "what would it mean for our industry if, in the foreseeable future, the basic cell phone could be smaller in size than a penny, and cost less than a dollar?" To be fair this was many years ago, but nonetheless, the most frequent responses I received, during and after this speech, were about why this was not likely to be possible, for various technical reasons.

I imagine that most of us would probably agree that being open-minded is a good thing, but the reality is that most of us aren't as open minded as we think we are. To demonstrate this, I have developed a very simple exercise that I often conduct with audiences I meet. I call it the "paper clip exercise". I start by talking generally about why it is important to be open-minded. I then ask if there is anyone in the audience who isn't open-minded. This usually gets some giggles but no-one ever raises their hand. I then ask them to take the paper clip they were given when they entered the auditorium and to place it in one hand or the other, turn to the person sitting next to them and ask them to guess in which hand they placed the paper clip.

Everyone is asked to take a turn doing this, and I then ask for a show of hands to see how many were able to guess correctly. It usually turns out to be about 50/50.

Most people will place the paper clip in one hand or the other and close their fists in such a way that the other person cannot see which hand the paper clip is in. It comes as a surprise when I demonstrate to the audience that what I asked them to do was simply to put the paper clip in one hand, I never said anything about closing the hand. I never said it was a contest or that there were any consequences to the results of this exercise. In fact, I intentionally gave very little information about the purpose of the exercise.

As it turns out, most of us have references in our minds from early childhood when we played guessing games with our parents. When we are confronted with a new assignment such as the paper clip exercise, our brain automatically tries to make sense of the assignment. Our thought processes use what little information is available and look for patterns of similarity within the references stored in our brain. In this way, we access past knowledge or experience to help us understand, and successfully manage, the new situation.

There is really no way for most of us to stop our brains from doing this pattern search. Our brain is doing what it is designed to do. Our brains are incredibly efficient and our capacity to sort through enormous quantities of data to find meaningful references is incredible. But after having drawn conclusions regarding the current situation's similarities with our knowledge and past experience, we also need to reflect upon ways in which this new challenge differs from these. At some level, every new situation is unique. No two situations will ever be exactly the same. Sometimes, two situations are close enough that the differences are negligible and we can easily 'copy/paste' a solution into the new situation. Sometimes, the differences are significant enough to require at least some level of innovation.

For much of our daily life, it is helpful that we have fixed ideas and preconceived notions about the world around us. You might argue that the process of growing up and becoming educated is a process of becoming less and less open-minded. When we are small children, it is just as easy for us to believe that the moon is made of cheese as it is that rain is wet. As we grow and learn, we exclude these childish notions from our realm of possibilities and again, this is a good thing.

I discovered this when my youngest son was learning his multiplication tables in primary school. One day, we were using flash cards and I showed him 4 x 8 = ?. He thought for a moment and said "647". I looked at him with desperation in my eyes and asked him how he could possibly come up with an answer like 647? He looked at me with his big blue eyes and said "dad, don't you know that numbers are infinite?" At that moment, I realized how completely open-minded he truly was. At that point in time, he hadn't yet grasped the concept of multiplication. He was just learning the multiplication tables. All he really knew was that one number times another number was equal to a third number. So the problem

4 x 8 = could be any number from zero to infinity. Since he didn't know the right answer, any number had the same chance of being the right answer. After a short time, he mastered his multiplication tables and the answer to 4 x 8 will forever and always be 32 and nothing else. This is a good thing. It is good that we learn from experience and are able to apply and adapt our knowledge to new situations. But sometimes, we need to disengage that process in our brains and look at a situation with new eyes, which are not limited by past experiences.

When I was the head of the cell phone business in Sweden for Telia Corporation, I found myself in a discussion with several engineers about how we could deliver a specific new service to the market. I was becoming increasingly frustrated because they were telling me that what we wanted to do was impossible. Since I am not a telecoms engineer, I was at something of a technical disadvantage, so I asked them what they meant by "impossible". Did they mean that our idea went against the laws of physics? They replied that what we wanted to do didn't conflict with the laws of physics but that it was very, very difficult. Then I asked them if they could solve the problem if they had all the money in the world and all the people in the world available. They looked at me with that tired look only an engineer can give to a dimwitted general manager and said that, of course they could fix this new service under those circumstances.

Finally, I asked them whether creating this new service would require all the money in the world and all the people in the world. If the actual resources that were needed weren't equivalent to everything in the world, approximately how much resource would be needed? As it turned out, what my colleagues meant by "impossible" was that it was outside of the normal framework of resources within which we were accustomed to working. When we worked out the business case and presented it to our executive management, the team approved the investment and that service became an important part of our service portfolio.

The following is a list of ideas managers could implement to improve the creativity from within an organization.

1. Don't be afraid of conflict. Encourage constructive conflict. When it comes to creativity, there is a great deal to be said in favor of a healthy dissonance. As long as disagreements are focused on ideas, and not on the people behind the ideas, creativity will bubble. Do not tolerate aggressive or rude behavior. Develop an atmosphere where dynamic, passionate, and even animated, discussion of ideas to improve your organization, products or services, is encouraged.

2. Let go for a while. Sometimes, when we work too long and hard on a specific challenge, we need to give our brain time to assimilate, analyze and rest. Work on something else for a while or take time off. While our conscious mind is thinking of something else or resting, our unconscious mind is sorting through all the information and impressions without us being aware of it. Unexpectedly, and out of the blue, our brains will make a breakthrough in the problem on which we have been working. I have often paused a difficult meeting and asked the participants to take a short walk with me.

3. Be playful and experiment with 'no limitations'. Sometimes, our creativity gets stuck in a rut. When we are working within the given structures of our organizations, processes and guidelines, project methodologies or technical environments we can come up with good ideas, but not exceptional ideas. Ask yourself questions such as "what would we do if we didn't have organizational, financial or technical limitations?" It might surprise you to discover that many of the ideas generated when thinking in this way don't actually require unlimited resources, just a little new thinking.

4. Experiment with having extremely limited resources as well. In the same way that you could fantasize about having

unlimited resources you can play with the idea of having extremely limited resources. Thinking about solutions with very limited resources often leads to a real breakthrough for non-conventional solutions.

Tips to help you make a fact-based decision

1. Insist on actual analyses and objective information.
2. Do not confuse anecdotes with facts.
3. Adjust everything to the situation! Learn from the past, but remember that you will probably never be faced with exactly the same situation twice.
4. If you have to use more intuitive information, make sure the information comes from the person or persons most qualified in the area.

COMMANDMENT 8

Say what you think:
create a climate where
others dare to do the same.

One mistake that most of us make at some time is not saying what we think. By that, I don't mean letting your own viewpoints dominate the discussion, or attacking other people's ideas. What I mean is that you have earned a position because you have certain qualifications and those are what you must communicate and express. We are not paid to do what managers say, we are paid to think for ourselves, reason, analyze, question and come up with sensible conclusions. That is our duty, both as employees and managers: to say what we think is best for the enterprise.

In Commandment 1, I presented the problem of 'yes-men' from a manager's standpoint, but there is another side where you, as a manager, must dare to say what you think – or there is a risk that you, yourself, will become one of the yes-men. Instead of driving forward, growing and developing the organization, you will become a part of the organization's stagnation. When I used the example of my son who did not dare to tell his teacher he thought her classes were boring, you could say that he contributed to her continued poor teaching by not telling her what he thought. It is understandable that a small boy could not bring himself to criticize his adult teacher, but it is unacceptable that adults in senior positions, within the same organization, do not say what they think, out of fear or apathy.

At this point, I would like to raise a warning finger regarding the growing culture of *positive thinking* that has become so popular in recent years. I am not opposed to positive thinking. I am a fairly optimistic person myself and I think that most of us would rather be around people who are positive. And people who see opportunities in every problem can be fun to be around. But there are several problems related to this approach. One problem is that, in their determination to build a positive culture in their companies, many managers unconsciously create an atmosphere where people do not dare to bring up problems or point out risks in the company and its strategies. President George W Bush was a firm believer in positive thinking and had a tendency to interpret people with differing views as naysayers. As a result, Condoleezza Rice, his Secretary of State, did not dare to speak out about the obvious risks inherent in invading Iraq.

Another problem inherent in believing too strongly in positivism is that many talented people who are not positive in nature, but who have skills that can be decisive for the company they work for, do not get enough attention or appreciation. In his book *The Happiness Hypothesis*, Jonathan Haidt explains that research indicates that approximately half of us are born with a more pessimistic attitude. According to researchers, there are strong biological reasons for this division among the population. The half of the population that sees the glass as half full needs the other half that sees the glass as half empty (and vice versa) in order to succeed.

I like to use the TV series *House* as an example. If you have seen it you certainly will remember the lead character, a medical doctor, Dr House, who is an exceedingly difficult, egotistical, complex person with enormous problems. But he is also a brilliant diagnostician who manages to identify, and usually cure, one unusual disease after the other. If I ever contract a terrible illness, I hope there is a Dr House in the house. The character of Dr House is exaggerated, but I have often worked with people who are not very skilled socially and who can be extremely negative, but whose competence and world view has always contributed to a healthier and more successful organization.

The fact that I caution against excessive positivism does not mean that I advocate pessimism.

Pessimism has deficiencies that are the opposite of the problems of positivism; for instance, it can lead to underestimating opportunities and over-exaggerating risks. Instead, I advocate realism. It is only when you look at yourself, the company, and the world around you as realistically as possible that you can develop and implement strategies that will work in the short term and the long term. People in all enterprises run into problems and face all kinds of tough challenges, and without a realistic approach, there is a good chance that they will over- or under-estimate both the difficulties and their own ability. For a more detailed study of this, I would recommend reading the book *Smile Or Die* by Barbara Ehrenreich, which takes a look at the truths and myths of positive thinking.

One method I have used to encourage more negative or critical viewpoints has been to add a special point for them to the meeting agenda. When I was the vice president of marketing at TeliSonera, I had a group of gifted employees. These people were extremely talented in their own disciplines and performed at a high level. But they could also be really whiny. I have often thought that a bi-product of being so gifted is the ability to see so many flaws in the organization.

Nevertheless, these flaws caused a great deal of irritation for these people, and for the most part, the complaining formed part of the office chit chat. I caught snippets about this, that and the other. One day, when we were going to have a group meeting with the entire department, I added a point to the agenda that I called "bitching and complaining". When my staff noticed that point on the agenda, there was some sceptical chuckling throughout the room, but I continued. I told them that I felt there was a fair amount of complaining and that I wanted to do something positive with it.

We started by gathering all the complaints and writing them on a whiteboard. It took some time to get everyone to dare to add their thoughts, but in the end it grew to be fun. Once we had written about 20 items on the board, we went through and discussed which of these had a major impact on the company, and which were simply minor irritations; those issues we could resolve easily, those which were more difficult, and those which could not be fixed at all. We realized, for example, that complaining about the overall economic downturn was understandable, but also a waste of time, because we couldn't do anything about it. But once we had worked through the list, we decided we should solve several of the easier, yet irritating, small issues and we started various projects or initiatives to remedy some of the larger ones.

Bitching and complaining is important to the value-creating process, as long as you don't get bogged down in it. It is and useful part of identifying and defining a problem.

If you perceive that something in your organization is on the verge of going wrong, tell someone. If you think the strategic plan is not good enough, tell someone. .....and back it up. If you have skills and knowledge that can advance a project, communicate this, so your colleagues can derive the benefit of your knowledge. Offering good advice after the fact is not good leadership. You are not a leader because you have hindsight. Bear in mind Commandment

2 about humility and not having all the answers, but when you do have insight that can have a significant impact on the organization, it is your responsibility to share it.

The same thing applies where an employee comes up with an idea or points out risks and dangers to you as a manager, and you take this into account when you make a decision. If the result is not what you expected, then it is an ordinary mistake, based on the reasoning put forth in the previous chapter. But as a manager, if you:

- make a bad decision because your staff have not given you the information and perspectives they possess, those staff members are just as much a part of that bad decision. In that case, they too have to accept part of the responsibility and not blame something or someone else
- do not ask for your staff's viewpoints, or if you create a climate in which employees do not dare to come forward with their opinions, and as a result you make a bad decision because you lacked vital input from them, the responsibility for that bad decision is yours alone.

I have been involved in situations in which a project has been headed for failure, where someone in the group had observed ways to improve the situation at an early stage but kept these to himself until it was almost too late. On one occasion I was on the verge of exploding while I was pointing out to the person in question that he had not done his job. He was made a member of the project group to use his head and not withhold his knowledge. Not to do so was irresponsible and verging on fraud!

Regardless of the particular job we have, we are paid to share our knowledge and our judgment, to suggest improvements, to dare to take risks, and to communicate our perceptions.

The same applies to all employees in an organization, but it applies even more for managers. It may be risky to say what you think, but as I discussed before, risk is a condition of success. As a manager, you have to say what you think and strive to help others do the same.

There are companies and managers that do not encourage employees to share their opinions. In spite of this, you should offer your viewpoints even though you know that no-one is listening or that they will not be well received. But at least you will have done your job and accepted responsibility. You cannot be responsible for how other people in the company do their jobs, but at least you have done yours.

In a modern organization, everyone (in particular managers) works to create an open atmosphere that enables staff to speak their minds. These days, organizations are more complex than ever before. This may be a geographical complexity, where employees belonging to the same organizational unit are located all over the world; it could be complexity in the form of organizationally hybrid solutions, such as matrix organizations, in which a large number of employees have a responsibility within several organizational units, or virtual organizations such as outsourcing. The increased complexity places high demands on anyone who offers his or her input. We see, and experience, the organization from various perspectives and viewpoints. In order to create a complete overall perspective, everyone must participate and contribute their own knowledge and competence from their unique point of view. All organizations and bosses need input; they cannot succeed purely as a result of their own talents and knowledge.

It is easy to lay the blame on your boss if you feel that no-one is listening to your opinions. But I maintain that our chief loyalty at work must be to the company as a whole and not to the person who happens to be the boss. If we see problems or identify opportunities for improvement, we have to proffer them.

Normally, we would turn to the manager responsible for that part of the company, but you can speak openly about your opinions and suggestions with other people as well. You have to respect the fact that the organization may make other decisions, or choose other directions, to the ones you have proposed. For most people, this is completely acceptable and something they tolerate. If you find it difficult to accept, you have to decide whether or not you want to stay.

Once, I was at odds with my boss about an important business decision. In order to arrive at a solution, we sat down, one afternoon, in a small conference room and argued, at times heatedly, for and against our varying standpoints. The discussion was lively and after a couple of hours my boss said:

"Kelly, I hear what you are saying, but I have to make a decision and we are doing it my way."

I was not surprised that he chose his own line. The subject was a minefield and we had discussed it so much that I felt that I wanted to show my loyalty, so I said to him:

"You know I think you are wrong, but from now on, I will do everything I can to prove you are right."

I felt that he had shown me respect, listened to what I had to say, and understood my viewpoints, but he simply did not agree with me. It was then my professional responsibility either to go along with his decision or to find something else to do. For my part, staying and half-heartedly supporting his decision was never an option.

If you feel you cannot stay in your job because you do not support the direction and decisions of the organization, or you have a boss who does not appreciate his or her employees giving their opinions, here is a good question to ask yourself: "What is the worst that can happen?" Maybe it is that you lose your job and become unemployed. You can comfort yourself knowing that you simply do not belong there. By that, I mean that the company does not deserve you and your competence. But there are few places of work where you risk getting fired for offering an opinion or viewpoint that differs to your manager's. It is conceivable that your boss will show his displeasure, but you are not risking much more than that. Personally, I would not like to work somewhere I was not allowed to voice my opinion or express my views. Regardless of how much money I was making. I would not enjoy it and would not do a good job in that kind of atmosphere. It would be so discouraging; I would find it tough to drag myself to work every day. But if management has genuinely listened to what I had to say I can live with them not always doing things my way. And that, I think, is how most people feel.

Most organizations want to create an open atmosphere, where employees dare to voice their opinions and criticisms freely. But many managers unwittingly create barriers that dissuade team members from offering up their opinions. As a leader, you are responsible for ensuring that both you and your employees can be heard. At times, you may have to put your ego aside, for a while at any rate, in order for your employees to dare to tell you what they think.

A boss who succeeds in creating an open atmosphere is one who asks his employees honestly what they think and lets them reply freely.

I have often seen managers ask for their employees' opinions only to tell them their own viewpoint in the very next breath. It is perfectly fine to tell your organization "we are faced with a challenge that is demanding and difficult" and to ask "what do you think we should do?"

And then to stay quiet and just listen.

The other thing a manager can do is delegate decisions. Our normal management jargon asserts that the boss makes the decisions and this viewpoint seems to be supported by a great deal of books and magazines on the subject. I, myself, have frequently been guilty of stating that managers make decisions, both in my everyday language and even in this book. But this way of looking at management is faulty. Delegating a decision does not mean that a manager does not stand behind the decision. It means he or she dares to trust his organization.

The manager's job is not to do everything on his or her own; he or she has to make sure the work gets done and to create opportunities and the conditions for others to do their jobs. The manager's job is not to make decisions; it is to ensure that the necessary decisions are made in the best possible manner, and more often than not, this means that someone other than the manager is making the decision.

In Richard De Charms' book, *Personal Causation*, he says that people "constantly battle against being controlled and restricted by external forces – against being moved around like pawns in situations they themselves have not chosen". It may seem self-evident that the greater control and influence we can give employees over their work and their lives, the greater their commitment to their work will be.

Sometimes, I ask managers who are constantly at the forefront, to formulate a question, give employees a framework, or define the limitations, and then let their team members work undisturbed on an assignment. Sometimes, it takes an hour, sometimes a day, and in some cases, a week or a month. The manager must be available throughout the process as a sounding board, and for support, but not necessarily present – which is sometimes an advantage.

The third, and perhaps most important, thing you can do as a manager, is to recruit competent staff and continue to invest in their skills development. In order to succeed in this, you must be able to rely on your staff. If you cannot, you have not recruited the right people; those to whom you can delegate duties and whose abilities and conclusions you can trust.

As a leader, you create the optimum conditions for your employees to be heard and enable them to vent their opinions, by being present but not interfering. Be sure to recruit skilled and competent people who are motivated and eager, and then let them get on with things. Remember Commandment 2: as a manager, you do not need to have an answer for everything.

Tips to help you create an open atmosphere

1. Stick to substantive issues, but always say what you think and accept the consequences.
2. Encourage others to say what they think, especially things that seem a little negative, and create routines and structures in order to take them seriously.
3. When you, or one of your decisions, is under criticism, do not become defensive. If you do, apologize and encourage further criticism.

COMMANDMENT 9

Support your staff:
remember, they work for
you of their own free will.

In an ideal world, we would all have chosen our jobs of our own free will, partly because we enjoyed the work and felt supported by our managers, and partly because we were in agreement with the company's objectives and direction. We would have made a conscious choice and been happy with it.

In reality, many people feel they are not working of their own free will in the jobs they have right now. They feel they have to work in order to have enough money to support themselves and lead decent, comfortable lives. This is a common notion. You could take this a step further and say that we are not forced to work; working is just a consequence of the society in which we live. We probably wouldn't starve if we didn't work, but life would not be much better than that. If we choose not to live in poverty, we have to work, but we do not have to work in anything in particular. We don't need to have a certain job, be employed by a particular company, or even think that what we are doing is especially interesting or fulfilling. That may be desirable for both you and your employer, but it is not necessary.

If everything in life were to fall apart, we could choose to take any job at all just to have an income. I usually say that if everything blows up in my face, I can always work at McDonald's. When I have been there with my children, I have noticed that the hamburger chain is almost always looking for staff and it seems to have a high staff turnover. I mentioned this in a talk once, and someone in the audience said:

"Kelly, there isn't a McDonald's that would hire an old guy like you."

So I went to a McDonald's and asked the manager: "Is it true that you wouldn't hire a 50-year-old geezer like me?"

He laughed and said there weren't many people of my age who were looking for work with McDonald's, but they would certainly appreciate a few older staff members because they usually stay in the job longer. He explained that many young people see work with McDonald's as something temporary and are often on their way to another job or further education. That is the reason for the high staff turnover. He added that he would definitely hire someone like me, so with that, I proved my hypothetical theory.

But I still struggle with the question of whether we actually work where we work of our own free will.

Of course, there are people in society who are involuntarily unemployed; people who, for various reasons, have difficulty entering the job market. And many who succeed in finding a job may not be working at something they really want to do. Without becoming too philosophical, I would still like to point out that *to want* something is a conscious act that requires consideration and reflection; it does not happen without thought. Quite often, unconsciously, we find ourselves doing things in life that are not what we really want. We don't necessarily do things we don't want to do consciously, but we may not have given much thought to what we really do want to do. You slide into a job, the years fly by, and one day you wake up and wonder how you got there.

To be fair to the subject, we could enter a long and difficult discussion of whether or not free will even exists. Scientists and philosophers have struggled for centuries over the question of free will. We may never know whether our actions are ultimately the result of our genes, our socialization (the result of things that happen to us and mold us throughout life) or the inner workings of our psyches, struggling to resolve inner conflicts. In all likelihood, what we call free will is a combination of many factors.

This is not a book on neuroscience, psychology or philosophy; this book has a more pragmatic focus on how we actually practise leadership. In short, what works and what doesn't. If, as some determinists argue (believing that, for every event, there is a set of conditions so that no other event could possibly occur), we do not have free will and our behaviors and decisions are already programmed into our genes or our psyches, then reading this book, or any book for that matter, might have no effect on our behaviors at all. In that case no harm done.

If, on the other hand, we assume a certain level of free will, then sharing ideas and learning from one another can contribute to modifying our behaviors . If a group of people were exposed to an outside threat like an earthquake, determinists would argue that whether we hide under our desks or run out in the street is a pre-programmed behavior, so providing earthquake-safety training would only be of any value if people were able to make their own decisions. That said, it would not have any negative effects on people with no free will, so the most practical solution is to assume that people do have free will. It is practical for us to assume that we have at least some capacity to make decisions and change our fate.

Many years ago, a man approached me after I had given a speech; he was somewhat irritated. He explained that life was easy for me with a highly paid, exciting job, while he himself had a dull job and poor pay. He described, in detail, his conditions of work and how awful his job was and continued to express his frustration at how poorly he was paid. When he was finished, I said that if I understood him correctly, he had worked for 15 years in a job he hated, and on top of that, he was poorly paid. He said that was correct. Then I asked him, "why?"

To my mind, the only logical motivation for someone to stay in an awful job would be an extremely high salary. But if you have an awful job and bad pay too, why do you remain? Why not find something else to do? After we chatted for a while, it became apparent that he never seriously considered what he really wanted to do. A friend of his had helped him get the job after he graduated from school, and 15 years later he was still there. Only recently had he begun to realize how much he disliked it. When I asked him what type of work or job he would rather have, he had no idea. A few years later, I received an email from him in which he told me that he had just graduated from college, started a new job, and was optimistic about the future. Sometimes, we all need to stop and ask ourselves what we are doing. Why we are doing it? What do we really want to do?

At some point, most of us have had a job that was not our dream job. When we were young, we may have taken a job just to pay for college or to get into the job market. I had many jobs like that when I was at university. When I went to Sweden, I took a number of boring jobs just to get into the Swedish job market. My first few years in Sweden were pretty exciting and fun on a personal level, but extremely tough in terms of work. The most common objection I heard was that my Swedish was not good enough, although oddly enough, it was often from people who had not actually spoken with me; they had only seen my resume and cover letter.

Often, I received a letter politely thanking me for my application, but stating that it was important that I was proficient in Swedish... again, despite the fact that I hadn't even been called to interview. At one point, I phoned the employer and asked how they could decide my Swedish was not good enough without having spoken to me. I always had my job applications checked by several native Swedes before sending them off and they were as good as flawless. For several years, I didn't get the jobs I wanted, but in spite of this, I chose to work. What was important was that I made a choice; that I decided my own fate and did what was needed to enter the labor market. The challenges that confronted me were still minor compared to what many other people face.

After 30 years, Sweden is still a country that has difficulty accepting skills and expertise from 'non-typical' Swedish groups, despite Sweden's politicians struggling to overcome these inequalities. Meanwhile, each individual must accept responsibility for his or her own fate and make their own decisions about what they want to do.

Once you have decided to take charge of your own working life or professional career, you can establish a plan to change or improve your situation.

This plan could include taking lowly jobs as stepping stones to bigger and better things, or taking training courses to improve yourself. People who feel they are making conscious decisions, for which they take responsibility, are happier and more motivated than people who live with a victim mentality. Victims do not go to work because they want to; they feel life has hoodwinked them or they have had bad luck that forces them to work. This is reflected in their achievements and motivation. By making them aware that it is they, alone, who makes their choices and decisions, we are helping them take control of their own fate. Instead of simply being carried along by life, they make their own conscious choices.

People who have taken control of their own lives go to work every day because they want to. They decide they want to work for you and not for someone else. They decide whether they want to work at this company or not. No-one makes the decision for them or forces them.

I once presented to a number of executives from an industrial company and told them that employees work in their jobs, and for organizations, of their own free will. What is implicit in this is that they can decide not to work for you and also decide not to do what you say. One delegate put up his hand and said that he did not agree with me. He claimed that the staff had to do as he said because he was their boss.

"Do they really?" I asked.

"Yes, they have to."

I asked him to expand on his reasoning, and he said: "For example, we have to rinse the floor in part of the production area at regular intervals. It is a boring and tedious job that no-one really wants to do, but they have to do it because I tell them to."

"Do they really have to?" I repeated.

"Yes, of course they do."

"But if they don't rinse off the floor, what happens then?"

"They will get fired!"

"So they don't actually have to do it then."

The man looked irritated but could not come up with a retort. I added that, naturally, there are consequences to everything a person does, but that his employees were not forced to rinse off the floor in the production area. They could choose not to do it, stand by their decision, and take the consequences. In that way, they have made their own decision.

From a leadership perspective, it is important to understand that employees not only choose to work for you, they also choose whether or not to follow you as a leader.

This is where you have to be careful to distinguish between the terms manager and leader. An employee may not have chosen his job because you are the manager and leader, but because of the specific duties of the job, the direction of the company, or even the structure of the organization. Even if an employee doesn't regard you as his leader, he can show you a measure of respect. The employee does what is required of him, but at the same time may consider you to be a lousy, or even useless, manager – but not to the point that he cannot stand it.

In many instances, employees may not initially choose us as bosses, they choose a job they think is interesting, but as they get to know us as managers they can 'unchoose' us. Sometimes, an employee chooses a job because of the positive impression they have of the new boss. They come to the conclusion that they really want to work with this manager. Sometimes, it can be the other way around. What does a manager think about when recruiting staff? Many managers have the attitude that they, themselves, choose an employee and they do not consider that it is just as much the employee who decides whether they want the position and whether they want to work for them.

I was in that very situation myself when I was recruited as a product manager at Whirlpool. I went through a long recruitment process, involving several interviews and tests. In the end, I was contacted by the company HR manager who said that they were going to recommend me for the position to the senior executive who would be my immediate superior. By this point I had met a number of different people in the company, but not the person who was going to be my boss.

A few days later, I walked into his spacious, impressive-looking office, which had a couch and two easy chairs. He sat in one of the chairs and I was seated on the couch, facing him. He greeted me but was not particularly friendly and hardly looked at me. He was holding my CV in his hand and he flipped through it, almost as if he were bored. With a nonchalant gesture he let the CV fall to the floor and said: "Ok, why should I hire you? I can find hundreds of people with a resume like yours."

I was caught off guard, almost shocked by his attitude and question, and the only thing I could say was: "I thought that you only needed one person."

The interview was fairly dull and I thought the manager was strange and difficult. I left the office and was convinced I would not get the job. If I did get it, I was sure I didn't want it. I really didn't want to work for a company with a boss like that. I thought he was anything but likable.

The very next day, the HR manager phoned me and said that my potential boss was very impressed with me and offered me the job.

"Thanks, but no thanks," I answered, surprised. "I don't want to work for a person as unpleasant as him."

The HR manager explained that this particular manager could be a little hard-headed, that he had his own way of doing things in various situations, but that most people liked him as a boss, even if he could be difficult in the beginning. I was caught between a rock and a hard place. I really wanted the job, but I was dubious about working for this person. In the end I took the job and I never regretted it.

After a few months, as I got to know my manager, I found we got along well, and in fact, became friends. One night, when we were over at his place chatting, I asked him why he was so unfriendly and arrogant during my interview, to the point that I almost turned down the job.

"You already had the job, but I wanted to see if you had thick skin and could handle a little adversity because the job can be tough at times."

Although the company and the manager had chosen me, they were surprised that I almost declined the offer because of the manager. Ultimately, both sides got to choose.

So how do I, as a leader, make sure that the employees do not 'vote me out'? You have to create the conditions under which people want to work with you, for a common purpose, towards the company's goals. To ensure that it will work, clarify the company's goals so the employees are aware of them and feel they are goals they want to work towards. In fact, it is preferable if they create the goals themselves. If I succeed, I will be helping the employees enjoy what they are doing. If an employee finds that he or she is not enjoying his job, he or she has a responsibility to create the job he or she wants, or to find it. In the end, if a person chooses to work with me, he or she has also demonstrated their intent to collaborate and help the organization to achieve its objectives.

Let's say that I want to start a company involved in selling toothbrushes for dogs and dog dental hygiene. It's not long before I need some help, so I advertise for a salesperson. The people applying for the job know that we work with dental hygiene for dogs and selling doggie toothbrushes. If a person applies for the job, that means they can see themselves supporting our business idea. If that person accepts the job, we are in agreement that, together, we will work to improve dental hygiene for dogs and strive to develop that market.

Suppose, after a few months, the new employee suggests that we should sell sticky notes instead. There is a huge need for them and an enormous market. I realize that sticky notes might be a good business idea, but not for this company. The employee has every right to sell sticky notes, but not here. It would be better for the salesperson to find another job, and for me, as manager, to hire someone else who supports the company's direction and objectives. As a manager and a leader, I understand how important it is for my employees to want to work with me, and it is crucial that I create the conditions needed for them to want to do so.

This way of seeing the roles of manager and staff is far from the 'command culture' where the manager gives the orders and employees do his or her bidding. The wise manager has understood that employees do what they want and not what the manager tells them to do. The secret is that we both have to want the same thing.

Tips to help you support your employees

1. Discuss with your employees why they chose their jobs. What was it that attracted them to the role or company in the first place, and what keeps them here? That reminds staff that it was their decision to take the job and gives valuable insight into what drives them.
2. Be clear in communicating the purpose, objective, and visions of the company and think about why staff should go along with these.
3. Identify specific measures and activities in order to align the employees' interests with those of the company.

COMMANDMENT 10

Go from manager to leader:
the company chose you as boss
but your employees decide
whether you are their leader.

For most people, it is obvious that a manager and a leader are not one and the same. You can be a manager without being a leader and a leader without being a manager. But what is the difference? First and foremost, being a manager is a position and leadership describes a relationship. In most cases, the organization appoints the manager and gives them formal and legal authority within the company, which entails a certain amount of responsibility. Management involves assuming responsibility for personnel, having greater freedom to make decisions and to achieve the best results possible. But, while the manager holds the formal authority associated with a certain position, it is the employees who choose who to follow as leader, and who holds the informal authority. They will decide, of their own accord, whether they will follow you, regardless of whether you are their manager or not.

In an organization where the manager is not secure in his or her role or leadership, it shows; he or she may even be afraid of the employees who are leaders, but not managers. This becomes even more obvious in organizations where people are expected to act as leaders without being managers. It has become much more common for organizations to remove the formal personnel responsibility that used to be typical for middle managers and retitle these positions as 'team leaders' or something similar. This new trend is not always a good thing as it is often driven by a desire to use middle-management positions to keep management salaries low, which, in some cases, can result in rather absurd corporate practices. For example, I have seen situations where a number of department manager positions were eliminated and the departments where consolidated into a larger working unit. This meant that the people in the group reported to a new managerial role with responsibility for all the people. This new managerial role was responsible for everything the old department heads used to do like salary discussions, performance reviews, recruiting, and planning. One practical advantage of this was that managerial costs were radically reduced from multiple managers to just one. It didn't take long for the disadvantages to show up. Many of these new managers had between 50 and 100 people reporting directly to them. The shear burden of administration left no time at all for leading. One of these new managers told me, "I don't know how I am expected to have a personal development discussion with each employee twice a year, I can't even keep track of all their names." Ultimately, the old department heads were retitled as "team-leaders" and assumed most of the old responsibilities they had had as department managers, except that they no longer had the compensation benefits that accompanied the department manager role.

For instance, one of the most important parameters that influences salary levels for middle managers is the number of people who report to them. If you do away with the staff responsibility, you can justify giving middle managers lower pay. Then you refer to middle managers as team leaders and make it clear that they are still expected to lead their groups and achieve their results without the formal title of manager.

In this type of organization, other managers have 50-100 employees who formally report directly to them, but it is impossible to provide meaningful feedback and support to all these people. One manager who participated in one of my courses told me she had just over 100 employees reporting to her and that her organization had a requirement that every one of them must undergo a performance review twice a year. With a little desperation in her voice she said: "I have enough trouble remembering their names. There isn't a chance of keeping track of what they all do, and I can't give them any reasonable feedback."

Team leaders have their own objectives to meet just like every other member of the team, which means that something has to give. Either they focus on reaching their personal goals and neglect their role as leader, or they focus on leadership and let their individual objectives suffer.

Another factor that leads to more roles for leaders, without an increase in the number of management positions, is that the role of the specialist has gained greater importance. In some types of enterprise, specialists or experts have always had a special position and performed a kind of leadership function; for example, within the healthcare sector or in universities, where doctors and professors may have a leadership role without necessarily being managers.

Nowadays, it is much more common for an expert to take on the role of a leader in other areas of organizations as well. It could involve a technical specialist who assumes a more prominent role in a project or an account manager in order to secure a vital order from a customer. It is also more common for companiess to organize their work around projects, so project managers play a key role. The project manager is, as the name suggests, a manager who has the responsibility for leading a group of people for a limited period of time, in order to achieve a well-defined objective. The project manager, however, normally lacks formal managerial responsibilities in terms of the project participants. Training for project managers has mainly focused on teaching project methodology, and it is only in recent years there has been a greater focus on developing their leadership skills. Some of these informal leaders become so powerful that they create anxiety among managers, who feel insecure in their roles as leaders.

A manager who does not gain acceptance and is not perceived to be a leader by his subordinates will often decide not to promote an informal leader who has the trust of the employees.

These managers are usually afraid that other leaders will threaten their position. If they can overcome their fear and forget about their prestige, they would start becoming leaders themselves and support and promote other leaders who could be beneficial for the entire organization. Hesitancy and uncertainty in a manager will permeate the entire organization. That is why strong, talented leaders want to surround themselves with strong, talented leaders.

A newly hired manager in a company is not, automatically, a leader. Some organizations, however, have gone so far as to create their own 'lingo' replacing the word 'manager' with 'leader'. They do not hire new managers, they recruit leaders; they don't have management meetings, they have leadership conferences, and so on. You begin to wonder whether the hope is that if they call managers leaders often enough, they might actually become leaders.

When I became head of Telia Mobile in Sweden, that was the lingo we used, although to me, it sounded a little strange. When I joined, the personnel department assembled a few hundred employees to meet me, in a large auditorium. The personnel manager, who organized the event, introduced me by saying: "Please allow me to introduce our new leader, Kelly Odell!"

I was new at this company which meant I did not know any members of staff and they didn't know me. All that was generally known about me was what had been written in an article in Sweden's main business newspaper a few days previously, in which a reporter railed against me writing: "You planned to be a preacher and then you ended up selling fridges. What makes you qualified to lead Telia Mobile?" His angle seemed to be that I was totally incompetent.

Remaining mindful that no-one in the room knew me, other than through that article, it felt awkward and embarrassing to step up onto the stage and be hailed as their new leader. It would have been even more embarrassing had I taken the opportunity to cry out: "I'm your leader!"

In some way, I wanted to signal that I understood the rules of the game. So I thanked the HR manager for the introduction and said that, for the time being, I was simply their new boss and that, in time, I hoped I could live up to their expectations and become their leader, but that we would just have to wait and see. I felt I had to explain to people that the company had appointed me as their boss, an appointment I took very seriously, but the company could not appoint me leader. That was up to them, the employees.

At one point, after a major reorganization, I found myself in a new management group with a new boss. At our first management group meeting, a group of managers was sitting around a table. Most of us knew one another from other projects, but we did not know our new boss. He explained that he had handpicked each of us because, during the course of our lives, we had learned to be good leaders. He, on the other hand, was a born leader. Even as a child in the school playground, it was clear that he was a leader. Most of us could hardly restrain our laughter. He never became our leader, even after we had worked for him for a couple of years.

Sometime later, I ended up in a discussion with the same manager. We were in a management group meeting, during which it turned out that we had differing opinions about an important business decision. I thought we had had an open-hearted discussion but it turned out that I was entirely wrong about that. Suddenly, this manager slammed his fist into the table and cried out: "I AM THE BOSS!"

Everyone in the room was shocked by his outburst. I looked him in the eye and, when I finally could control myself, smiled and replied in a slightly condescending tone: "Yes, you are."

In the exact instant that he was exerting his authority as a boss with such emphasis, he lost all power as a leader. It was clear to me, and to everyone else, that he felt threatened, and lacked the ability to convince us of his view on the matter. In pure desperation, he clung fast to the fact that he was our boss.

The actual power in an organization, the power to influence and lead, has its origins in the motivation of your staff.

You cannot bully people into being motivated or inspired or lead by force. Some bosses think that an employee has to do what they say and anyone who doesn't will simply be fired. The boss doesn't realize that there is always a choice, that an employee can quit a job of their own free will. You cannot force someone to stay. By the same token, you cannot create leadership by claiming the formal power that comes from being boss. A boss has very simple and blunt power mechanisms at his or her disposal. They can fire an employee, but that doesn't happen very often.

They can influence the size of an employee's salary, but during my 30 years in various management positions, the available margin for pay raises has always been around 2%. In other words, you actually do not have that much power to wield as a manager/boss. True power comes when your employees decide to follow you and support you as their leader because they want to. That is when you can get things done with power and strength. The crucial power that enables you to have an impact on the company, change something for the better, and create something new, comes when staff say: "Yes, we support you!"

I believe that the day it dawns on today's managers that they derive true power and influence directly from their employees is the day they come to an insightful realization. The key is not their position. Once this realization takes root, it will change the actions and behavior of managers. We will see a leadership revolution, in which leaders begin to understand that they get their power from the people who follow them.

A manager is appointed in a relatively dictatorial process, while a leader is chosen by staff, in a silent, democratic process without a formal election. The leader who wins the hearts of his or her employees assumes more power, increased influence, and greater opportunities to have a say in the organization. The other power, the one that is legal and formal, accompanies the position, but has nothing to do with the employee's choice, which is the base of real power.

Tips to help you go from manager to leader

1. Ask yourself why your staff ought to accept you as their leader.
2. Focus on earning the trust and respect of your staff, not demanding it.
3. Think about the type of culture you would like to help create and the legacy you wish to leave after you are gone.
4. Define activities that create your legacy.

MYTHS ABOUT ORGANIZATIONS

AND THE PEOPLE WITHIN THEM

I n addition to the ten commandments I have presented in this book, there are a number of 'myths' about people and organizations that undermine our success as leaders. In this chapter, I will present a few of the myths that are most prevalent and dangerous.

Myths about Recruiting

If you have ever spent time reading employment advertisements you will have discovered that a very clear change has taken place over the past 20-30 years. In the 1980s, when I was first entering the workforce, employment ads were often ridiculously specific about the education and experience a candidate should possess. A typical ad might not only stipulate what you should have studied but with which professor. It might not only specify the types of work experience a candidate should have undertaken, but spell out the preferred companies, departments and positions.

But as with most things in the world of management, when the pendulum has swung far to one extreme, it is bound, eventually, to swing back to the other. Today, it is much more common for an employment advert to focus on personality traits and verge on nonchalance, regarding the candidate's actual knowledge or skills. Even for professions requiring very specific skills, for example engineering, it is not uncommon to see that applicants should be able to manage stress, be a team player and have great social skills. Companies such as Southwest Airlines in the US have built their success on the idea of "hire for attitude and train for skills". Everyone is looking for extroverts with a firm handshake and a big smile. Typical 'introvert' characteristics, such as shyness, a more analytical mind and a cautious attitude are not deemed to be positive personality traits.

While writing this book, I did a Google search of Google's job openings in San Francisco and found they were searching for software engineers who were "versatile, displayed leadership qualities and enthusiasm". I'm not going to argue that Google's approach is necessarily wrong for the company, but where does the gifted engineer who lacks the desire or qualities to lead fit in? How can you tell if someone is enthusiastic? If it is through some form of exuberant outer expression then where do the introverts fit in? Introverts can be enthusiastic, but it may not be as easy to notice, especially for a group of extroverts.

It is very common to use personality tests, such as the Myers Briggs test, during the recruitment process. With the help of these tests we can gain insight into the personalities of the candidates. Certainly, at an intuitive level, this might seem reasonable. What could be wrong with trying to hire people who fit in and who possess the 'right' personality traits in order to make the greatest contribution to our organizations? But the truth is that this approach can be detrimental to your business.

One major problem with having too much focus on personality is that very few of us in management positions actually know much about psychology. Psychology has become popular, and many people use the language of psychology all the time. The problem is that the human psyche is complex, and most of us have, at best, a basic understanding of the workings of the human mind. I frequently hear people describe their boss or a colleague as a 'psychopath', 'sociopath', 'narcissist' or something else. But I imagine most of us would be hard put to actually describe what these labels really mean and the differences between them. (Even researchers and psychiatrists debate the differences between these terms).

Some years ago, I was involved in the hiring process for a vice president position at Volvo cars. By the end of the process, we had identified a candidate who had all the right qualifications, a good education, significant experience in similar roles and excellent references. The candidate was genuinely likable and everyone who had met him during the interview process was impressed.

As a matter of routine, we gave the candidate a standardized IQ test and were shocked at the results. The candidate's analytical skills were far lower than anyone could have imagined. This led us to dig deeper with several of the candidate's references, and sure enough, with the right questions, the truth came out. All of the referees really liked the candidate and wanted to help him to his next position, but they admitted he had shown signs of poor judgment and weak analytical skills. This candidate had great social skills and a good attitude, both of which would be valuable in the position he was seeking, but we doubted whether he had the intellectual skills to handle the challenges this position would involve. In the end, we kept looking until we found another candidate.

Even had we succeeded, through personality testing, to match a candidate to the specific profile we had created, how would we, as hiring managers, have known the precise personality profile required? A psychologist at a recruiting company may have the skill to help us create a profile and identify people who match it, but they generally don't know much about the real requirements of various jobs or which profiles are needed in our culture. The cards are often stacked against the candidate in the recruitment process. Where there are a number of candidates, all of whom possess the necessary skill-set for a position, the evaluation process can easily become focused more on looking for reasons not to hire an individual than for reasons to hire them.

Used carefully, personality testing and other tests, such as IQ tests, may have value in screening out the wrong candidates, but are much less useful in identifying the right ones. My suggestion is to view characteristics such as personality traits, social skills or sexual/cultural diversity as a part of the skill-sets needed for a position. Although, strictly speaking, personality is not a skill, viewing it as a skill can help us put it into the proper perspective. For example, in the case of Southwest Airlines, good social skills and a positive mental attitude could be said to be key skills for the job. Other skills, including how to operate the ticketing system or to handle customer baggage could be taught on the job. If you were recruiting a brain surgeon, their technical skills would be the priority.

Personality or attitude can be valuable assets, as long as we view them as one parameter among many. But to adopt "hire for attitude, train for skills" as a general rule is a dangerous over-simplification.

Myths about Diversity

Another problem is that hiring managers tend to describe ideal candidates that are very similar to themselves. We tend to like people who are similar to ourselves and our ideals. In fact, the entire notion of 'good social skills' is extremely subjective. What I consider good social skills may be quite different from what you consider them to be. Many companies have focused in on the stereotypical 'cheerleader' profile believing that these energetic extroverts would be great for their businesses. There is no doubt that this type of profile can be perfect when dealing with some clients, suppliers and colleagues. But it is equally certain that others can perceive these people to be overbearing and pushy.

If research has taught us anything about high-performing teams, it is that diversity drives performance and lack of diversity kills it. Diversity drives performance in two main ways. First, and possibly most obviously, people from different backgrounds bring different ideas. They have experienced different ways of approaching and solving problems and this contributes a broader understanding of the possibilities available to us. Sometimes, the unique perspectives of people from diverse backgrounds can create immediate short-term benefits.

For example, the migration of people across the globe creates unique new sales opportunities. Many companies have discovered the benefits of hiring salespeople from similar cultural backgrounds to the customers they are targeting. Other benefits can take longer to realize but can be significantly more rewarding as in using diversity to help drive product innovation. The second way that diversity drives performance is that people from diverse backgrounds help to break down the 'truths' or biases that homogenous groups tend to hold.

Groups of people from similar cultural backgrounds have been raised in a common environment and tend to take certain elements of the world around them for granted. Everything, from what we eat and how we dress, to our values and how we prioritize and solve problems can, to a great extent, be affected by the cultural environment in which we have been socialized. But in order to improve and innovate in our organizations we must question our truths about the established way of doing things. Scott E Page, Professor of Complex Systems, Political Science and Economics at the University of Michigan, argues that when people are too similar, they are far less likely to see things that others have not already seen before (*The Difference*, 2008).

But although diversity is crucial to performance, recent research indicates that creating diversity within the group isn't sufficient to drive performance. You have to encourage interaction between the diverse members of the group. Chatting around the water cooler isn't as important as who you chat with at the water cooler. It is relatively easy for a manager to bring together individuals of differing sexes, ages or cultural backgrounds but it is much harder to get these individuals to really interact. There are significant barriers to interaction that should not be underestimated.

You only have to look at many organizations to see just how hard it is achieve real diversity. Even relatively simple forms of organizational diversity, such as gender diversity, can be extremely difficult to achieve. While today, women represent 47% of the US workforce, a recent study from the Pew Research Center showed women lag far behind men in terms of leadership positions – and the higher up in leadership you look, the worse the problem is.

In 2014, women represented only 22% of senior managers from mid-market businesses and approximately 5% of CEOs on the Fortune 500 corporations. This particular problem with diversity is relatively easy to resolve; we simply need to hire and promote more women to leadership positions. Women are easy to identify, and in today's workforce, they possess the right skills and experience to fill all the positions we need. So why don't we "just do it" to coin a phrase from Nike?

The simple answer is that it just isn't that simple. Society (including many women themselves) still has deeply ingrained beliefs and prejudices that make progress slow. According to PEW, a third of men and just over half (53%) of women believe that women are held to higher standards in top business positions than their male counterparts. The same study showed that 35% of men and 50% of women felt businesses just weren't ready to appoint women to top positions.

Both findings show what I would call 'cultural' barriers rather than 'structural' barriers. A structural barrier might be women lacking the necessary educational requirements or physical attributes for a certain job, while cultural barriers lie more in the perceptions of society and have nothing to do with the individual's ability to perform. Before we can generate real diversity of interaction between diverse individuals we need to make it possible for diverse individuals to gain positions at all levels within our organizations.

Myths about Creativity

Creativity is a fundamental necessity when it comes to identifying new business models and strategies, more effective ways of working, or developing exciting new products and services. Despite creativity being so critical to success in today's organizations, knowledge around creativity is often low and myths and misunderstandings abound.

As head of Whirlpool Corporation's national sales organization in Sweden, one of my responsibilities was to launch the Whirlpool brand name in the country, which was virtually unknown at the time. This meant participating in many meetings with our advertising agency to discuss plans. I was often entertained by the jargon the advertising agency used. For example, they referred to certain employees as "creatives".

Whenever I had meetings with these creatives they were almost always unshaven, dressed in black, and wearing ponytails and cowboy boots. At that time, a dark grey business suit with a tie was what I tended to wear to work, so you can understand the surprise of people at the ad agency when I showed up at one of our meetings unshaven, in jeans, T-shirt and cowboy boots. The room became very quiet, and for a moment, everyone stared at me. I said: "I see you've noticed my appearance; I thought that I might try to be creative today too."

The notion that creativity is a characteristic only some people possess is wrong. Everyone can be creative and most people are creative. Some people have just practised more and therefore seem to be more creative than others. Even if ideas do occasionally just pop into our heads from nowhere, creativity is more about hard work than it is about luck or magic. Hard work around a specific question or problem significantly increases the chances of identifying a creative idea.

If you work at it, brilliant ideas can sometimes come from unexpected places. In the early '90s, when I was the product manager for Whirlpool Corporations' microwave oven business in Europe, I came across a study that had been conducted with school children. The goal was to find out what features children would like to see in a microwave oven, to gain their ideas. One suggestion that came up several times in different focus groups was that the children wanted a microwave oven in their lunch boxes. That way, they could always eat warm food.

Of course, an engineer in our group swiftly pointed out how silly the idea was, since the transformer alone weighed several kilos. All the components for a microwave oven would be far too heavy for a child to carry around. However, another engineer explained that we didn't actually have to have a transformer in the microwave oven, we could use something called a switch mode power supply (SMPS), a small circuit board, weighing very little. The problem with the SMPS was that it was much more expensive than the transformer.

Someone else added that the SMPS shouldn't be that expensive, the main reason for the expense was probably just that we didn't buy them in large volumes. If we purchased SMPSs in as large a volume as we purchased transformers, they would probably be much cheaper than transformers. To cut a long story short, we never did develop a microwave oven that could be built into a child's lunch box, and to my knowledge, no-one else did either. What we did end up doing was replacing the transformers in our microwave ovens which resulted in better performance and functionality, better quality and less weight.

MY REFLECTIONS

L eadership is all about people, real people in real situations. I elected to use the term *human leadership* to clarify something I had hoped would be obvious. Leadership is practised by people, with people, and for people. This book is based on that obvious truth. To the best of my ability, I have tried to relate my experiences and reflections on how real people act and react in their roles as managers, leaders, and employees. People do not always behave perfectly, but they always behave like people.

Many people who become managers and leaders find it difficult to take the time for reflection. But I have had the benefit of being a teacher and speaker for many years. I remember well the first time I was going to speak at a conference as a contracted speaker. Speaking in front of a group was not new or unusual for me. I had always liked standing on a stage and had already made many presentations for work, and as a child, I performed often as a musician. The challenge was deciding what I wanted to say. It forced me to think about how I acted as a leader in various situations, what I was proud of in my behavior, and what I wished I had done differently. I realized there were too many examples of times when I was not proud of how I had handled a situation; there were even examples where I was downright ashamed. Of course, there was a great deal I was also proud of, and thanks to the lecturer and teacher roles, I was forced to take the time to reflect on both the good and the bad. As a result, I began changing many aspects of my leadership. I read and learned a great deal, experimented and grew as a leader. Thanks to this learning and reflection, I am a better leader today than I was yesterday and I hope to be even better in the future.

Someone once asked me what my eleventh commandment for leaders would be. After a brief moment, I replied that it would probably be along the lines of, "after you have finished reading my ten commandments, forget them and figure it out for yourself." Every individual is unique. This truth struck me once when

I dropped off my children at day care when they were very young. I heard one of the teachers say to one child, "you are unique." For some reason this struck me as amusing. It just sounded such a cliché.

I looked at the little boy to whom the teacher had spoken and thought "he looks pretty much like any other little boy his age, is he really unique or is that just the kind of meaningless thing we say to children without much thought?" But the reality is that we *are* unique. Each and every one of us is a unique individual. Right out of the starting blocks, each of us is endowed with a unique set of genetic building blocks. These building blocks help define our appearance, our intelligence, our health and our personalities. But these building blocks only give us our starting point. I will opt out of the 'nature versus nurture' debate, which in all likelihood misses the point anyway.

Who we are is not the result either of nature (genetic predisposition; what we are born with) or nurture (the individual's personal experiences). We are the products of both nature and nurture interacting together. As we gain experience, we learn, and learning is, in essence, a form of reprogramming our genetic starting point. From our very first breath, and most likely well before our first breaths, we are being formed by our environment. We not only experience different things throughout our lives, we also experience things differently. In short, no two human beings are exactly the same, and even when we are exposed to the same experiences, we are affected by these experiences differently. Even if every human being were born with exactly the same genetic starting point, by the time we became adults, we would still be entirely unique individuals due to the differences in our experiences. If we add to the mix that we are not born with the same genetic starting points, the potential for diversity becomes enormous.

So if no two people are the same, it stands to reason that no two leaders are the same. To complicate matters further, no two leaders will ever be in exactly the same situation. This does not mean we cannot learn from one another. We most certainly can, and do, learn from other people's experiences, but how we then apply what we have learned will depend on who we are and the specifics of the situations we face. The complexity of leadership lies not only in the fact that each of us, as a leader, is different, but also in each of the individuals we lead being unique. We can make generalizations about how human beings 'are', and how they act in various situations, but at an individual level, there is a great deal of variety of likely behaviors. It stands to reason that leadership is difficult and everyone makes mistakes.

My ambition has never been to write a comprehensive leadership manual. Having that as a goal would either suggest a level of arrogance on my part, or a fundamental misunderstanding of leadership as a subject (possibly both). I have asserted the thesis that leadership is a skill you can learn, but that you will never perfect. You have to practise continually and absorb new information, knowledge and experiences throughout your life. Research into leadership, and closely associated subjects such as motivation, are constantly marching forward and it is highly likely that parts of what we believe today will change over time, as new discoveries are made within a range of areas. What ultimately remains is the fact that leadership is all about people.

A Google search of leadership literature provides a jungle of publications, suggesting that leadership is simple and easy; many books actually include these words in their titles. The allure of such manuals is as understandable as it is dangerous. The fact that so many people struggle with leadership creates a desire to find simplifications and short-cuts. If leadership was that simple there would be no need for books describing it. When we over-simplify the complexity inherent in relationships, such as the relationships between leaders and followers, we miss important elements, and ultimately risk damaging the relationship. Good leaders have respect for the complexity of their role and accept that they will never master it completely.

Leadership teachings will undoubtedly develop over time, with new discoveries in behavioral sciences, organization theories, neuroscience, and genetics, and we, as leaders, must grow and develop in pace with the emergence of this new knowledge. Nevertheless, I believe there are a few things that will always be inherent in good leadership. Good leaders must be able to see themselves and others for who and what they are and not for what they want them to be.

Human beings are incredibly beautiful and exciting creatures, but also ugly and complex.

Good leaders must accept their roles as leaders with great humility and empathy and understand that to lead is also to serve. A leader should be seen but not stand in the way. A good example of this is found in the *Bible*'s New Testament: "But many that are first shall be last; and the last shall be first." (Mark 10:31).

The best leaders in history may have been those who were never seen. They appear seldom or never in history books and we do not know them. Their organizations may well have accomplished great feats without anyone really reflecting on the fact that there were one or more leaders who led them. The leaders in these organizations were colleagues and employees just like everyone else. The leaders were people with faults and weaknesses just like everyone else, but they mastered a professional role, the role of a leader. They developed the skills to lead and did it so well that no-one thought about there being a single leader. Success was attained because everyone's skills and competencies were accessible, because of the environment created by the leader.

Because leaders are ordinary people, good leaders know they need to listen carefully, to be open to criticism, and admit when they make mistakes, because everyone does at one time or other.

To be a human leader is to realize that you do not lead a company or football team, you lead people.

Being a human leader means you lead with human values. No matter what we learn from future research about leadership, the basic tenet about positive human values will prevail. Good leaders are genuinely interested in other people and see the purpose and objectives of the company as a tool for improving people's lives. Throughout history, there have been individuals with effective leadership skills, but who were not 'human leaders'; some were downright inhuman leaders. The human leader may well screw up, sometimes horribly, but they always strive to make the world better.

As I explained in the introduction to this book, my ten commandments for human leadership have been developed throughout my career. As I look back at them now you might even say that these commandments are in some way autobiographical in the sense that they mirror my own development as a leader. Early on in my career I realized that I was not willing to succeed as a leader at all cost. I knew that my own perceptions of success as a leader would only allow me to feel successful if that success was based on fundamental human values that were important to me. If I wanted to be successful in my own eyes and in the eyes of others I would have to rule my ego and not let it rule me... *Commandment 1 – Be humble.* I began to understand the importance of humility as a leader, that the leader was one of many important roles in a successful organization, not necessarily the most important. This led to the insight that if my area of expertise was to be as a leader I would need to learn to relinquish control and delegate responsibility to other people with other important competencies... *Commandment 2 – Dare to delegate.*

Success as a manager brought promotion, more responsibility and better compensation. I began to understand that there was also a backside to success. That, in fact, there was a very real risk that my success might ultimately lead to my failure. The very qualities of having nothing to lose and my willingness to take risks that made me successful early on in my career could be my undoing. I was becoming a part of something big and exciting and I wanted to remain a part of it. I was making a better living than I ever dreamed I would and I wanted more of it. All of a sudden I had a great deal to lose and my willingness to take calculated risks was declining and as a result my ability to stay on the success curve was eroding. I realized that if I wanted to stay on top I would have to maintain my freedom and keep taking risks... *Commandment 3 – Maintain your freedom and... Commandment 4 – Losing your job is not the worst thing that can happen.*

The higher I climbed up the corporate ladder the more frequently I was swept up in the politics and jockeying for power that is so prevalent in many organizations. I had to remind myself that any organization that prioritized internal politics above creating real value for the world around them would not be successful in the long-term and was not a place where I would want to invest my energy... *Commandment 5 – Deliver actual results.*

If my success as a leader was to be entwined with the organization's ability to achieve its purpose and goals under my leadership then I had to understand the mechanisms of motivation. How would I get people on board? How would I get them to do what I wanted them to do? The discovery that people ultimately do what they want, not what I want, was a turning point for me. My job was not to motivate but to inspire. I wasn't going to create motivation in my colleagues, they were already motivated. My job was to align people's interests around a common purpose. Success for me was going to be a matter of winning hearts as much as minds… *Commandment 6 – Be inspired and inspire others.*

Oddly enough, the higher I got into the corporate hierarchy the more surprised I was at the poor quality of the decision making process. Don't get me wrong, for the most part, when big decisions were being made there was a rigorous pack of information and analysis supporting it. The problem was that the weight of a single person's own experience or the impact of a witty story could outweigh months of tedious analysis. I came to understand that the world we live in and the organizations we lead are simply too complicated to rely too heavily on my "gut-feelings". If I was going to be successful I would have to respect the facts much more than my own intuition… *Commandment 7 – Base decisions on facts.* If I was going to try and see reality for what it was and not what I hoped it to be, I would have to be boldly honest in my own understanding and my communication with others. I would have to encourage the same behavior in others. My ability to create an environment where people were willing and ready to say what they thought, no matter the risk, would be crucial to the overall success of the organization… *Commandment 8 – Say what you think.* Finally, I came to the insight that the role of a good leader is that of servant. The role of the leader is to enable, empower, develop, facilitate and support so that the people in the organization can achieve the organization's purpose, not the individual purpose of its leaders… *Commandment 9 – Support your employees.*

Although I have heard discussions for years about the differences between managers and leaders, it wasn't until I began to understand the principles of motivation that it really sank in. All those years that I had been acting as a manager, I had only been tapping into the vein of extrinsic motivation which is shallow and complicated. My ability to truly lead would be defined by other peoples' willingness to follow me. If people choose to follow me, in essence allowing me to access their own significant well of intrinsic motivation then I could become an effective leader. I could not demand their respect as a manager, I would have to earn it as a leader. *(Commandment 10 – Go from manager to leader.)*

As time went by, I found that these commandments helped me align the needs of my staff with the goals and objectives of the organization as a whole. I discovered that the secret to success, and to achieving top results as a manager and a leader, was to understand and develop my personal values in relationship to the wants and needs of all the stakeholders of the organization. Summarised below are my ten commandments.

Commandment 1 – Be humble
Commandment 2 – Dare to delegate
Commandment 3 – Maintain your freedom
Commandment 4 – Losing your job is not the worst thing that can happen
Commandment 5 – Deliver actual results
Commandment 6 – Be inspired and inspire others
Commandment 7 – Base decisions on facts
Commandment 8 – Say what you think
Commandment 9 – Support your employees
Commandment 10 – Go from manager to leader

SUPPLEMENTARY MATERIAL

For links to leadership articles, models, templates, check lists and much more, visit **www.kellyodell.com**

ACKNOWLEDGEMENTS

I would like to thank my publisher Martin Liu, my editor Sara Taheri and the entire team at LID Publishing for their confidence in my book and their hard work and creativity. I would also like to thank Roger Kelly for his help in the early stages of preparing the manuscript.

REFERENCES

A P Buunk and NW van Yperen (1991)
Referential Comparisons, Relational Comparisons, and Exchange
Orientation: Their Relation to Marital Satisfaction. *Personality and Social
Psychology Bulletin*, nr 17, s. 709–717.

Richard De Charms (1968)
Personal Causation. Academic Press.

Edward L Deci and Richard Flaste (1995)
Why We Do What We Do: Understanding Self-Motivation. Putnam's Sons.

Deci, EL and Ryan, RM (1985)
Intrinsic motivation and self-determination in human behaviour.
New York: Plenum

Barbara Ehrenreich (2010)
Smile Or Die. Granta Books.

Malcolm Gladwell (2006)
Blink: The Power of Thinking Without Thinking. Prisma.

Daniel Goleman (1998)
Working With Emotional Intelligence. Bantam.

Jonathan Haidt (2006)
*The Happiness Hypothesis – Putting Ancient Wisdom to the Test of Modern
Science*. Basic Books.

John E Hunter, Frank L Schmidt and Michael K Judiesch (1990)
Individual Differences in Output Variability as a Function of Job
Complexity. *Journal of Applied Psychology*, nr 1 1990, 75(1):28–42.

Daniel Kahneman (2012)
Thinking Fast and Slow. Volante.

Sven Kylén (1993)
Work Groups with development and change assignments: from defensive to offensive routines. Psykologiska Institutionen, Göteborgs universitet.

Kevin R. Murphy (2006)
A Critique of Emotional Intelligence: What are the Problems and How Can They be Fixed? Lawrence Erlbaum.

Lee Ross (1977)
The Intuitive Psychologist and His Shortcomings: Distortions in the Attribution Process. *Advances in Experimental Social Psychology*, nr 10 1977.

Lyle M. Spencer Jr et al (1997)
Competency Assessment Methods: History and State of the Art. Hay/McBer.

Edward L Thorndike (1920)
Measurement of Intelligence. *Psychological Review*, 31(3), May 1924.

Rodd Wagner and James K Harter (2006)
12: The Elements of Great Managing. Gallup Press.

Christopher A (ed) Bartlett, Yves (ed) Doz, Gunnar (ed) Hedlund
Managing the Global Firm. Routledge

John Stuart Mill (Author), George Sher (Ed)
Utilitarianism, 2nd Edition

Scott E. Page (2008)
The Difference: How the Power of Diversity Creates Better Groups, Firms, Schools, and Societies

AN INTRODUCTION TO
KELLY ODELL

Author, speaker and management educator, Kelly Odell has spoken to audiences across the globe on change management, leadership and motivation always with a strong focus on execution. He has been hailed as a "master of metaphors" for his ability to transform complex concepts into simple, practical and actionable strategies.

A native of the USA, Kelly has worked in Europe for the past 30 years. Holding a degree in religion as well as an MBA he is sometimes called the "pastor turned businessman."

Kelly has many years of management experience in global corporations including president of Telia Mobile Sweden, senior vice President, Head of Group Marketing, for TeliaSonera Corporation, Managing Director for Whirlpool Corporation in Sweden and VP Sales Volvo Cars (Nordic). Kelly has received many awards as a public speaker and was highlighted by Veckans Affärer (a leading Swedish weekly business magazines) as one of Sweden's most influential foreigners.